Essays on Indian Diplomatic Dilemma in Nepal

Essays on Indian Diplomatic Dilemma in Nepal

Birendra P. Mishra

ADROIT

Adroit Publishers

NEW DELHI • KATHMANDU

ISBN : 978-81-87393-71-9

2019

Published by
ADROIT PUBLISHERS 4675/21, Ganpati Bhawan, Ansari Road, Daryaganj, New Delhi-110 002 Phone : 011-23266030
adroitpublishers@gmail.com

Typeset in Garamond Premier Pro by Arun, Akriti Graphic Solution, Delhi-110081 E-mail: arun263923@gmail.com, Ph: 9999414390

Dedicated to

My uncles who devoted their lives in politics:
1, Shyam Nandan Mishra, (in India),
2. Bhadrakali Mishra, (in Nepal),
3. Ram Narayan Mishra, (in Nepal).

Preface

India and Nepal are predominantly Hindu countries and there is goodwill among the peoples in abundance for hundreds of years. However, their formal relations hardly seem to be cordial, smooth and cooperative barring early 1950s. There are many political scientists and diplomats of Nepal and India who have expressed their views on Nepal-India relations exhaustively. They have dealt with the issues from their respective national perspectives. Finding their interpretations as partially true, I have strived to come up with my own views through this book, which may draw the attention of the stakeholders of Nepal and India simultaneously. Though there are several strong chains binding Nepal and India, the perspectives and strategies make them just opposite to each other. I have humbly endeavoured to look at the issue objectively to ascertain the causes leading to the present state of affairs.

John Whelpton, in his Foreword to Mandala Reprint Edition of 'Nepal Strategy for Survival' written by Leo E. Rose, writes, "...:an Indian absorption of Nepal would be a blow to China, but could in the long-run be lived with, as India lives with China's absorption of Tibet, but a Chinese takeover would be, in strategic terms, an absolute catastrophe for the Indian state." (1). He agrees with Rose that the key factors that have governed Nepal's relations with its neighbours in the past will continue to do so in the future.

The presupposition of John Whelpton will remain a hypothesis, as Nepal is careful about its existence as before. However, its slightest tilt towards any one side may jeopardize its balancing act. A foreign policy ought not be based on any one's whims and desires; it is rather based on historical facts and geographic positions and international conditions that guide its formation. More importantly, it must be followed by mature diplomacy.

Sometimes, diplomacy is erroneously confused with foreign policy. Diplomacy is a means to attain foreign policy, which establishes goals, prescribes strategies, and sets the broad tactics to be used in their accomplishment. It may employ secret agents, subversion, war, or other forms of violence as well as diplomacy to achieve its objectives. The purpose of foreign policy is to push forward a state's interests, which are derived from geography, history, economics, and the distribution of international power. The political leaders, who devise foreign policies, pursue what they perceive to be the national interest, adjusting national policies to changes in external conditions and technology. Diplomacy is the chief, but not the only, instrument of foreign policy, which is set by political leaders, though diplomats (in addition to military and intelligence officers) may at times advise them.

Yadunath Khanal, a scholarly diplomat of Nepal, defines diplomacy in brief. In his words, "...it becomes management of international relations by dialogue and negotiation." (2) Ernest Satow, a British scholar cum diplomat, defines diplomacy as, "the application of tact and intelligence to the conduct of official relations between the governments of independent nations," (3) Diplomacy is the principal substitute for the use of force or underhanded means in statecraft; it is how the comprehensive national power is applied to the peaceful adjustment of differences between states. The purpose of diplomacy is to strengthen the state, nation, or organization it serves in relation to others by advancing the interests in its charge. To this end, diplomatic activity attempts to maximize a group's advantages without the risks and expenses of using force and preferably without causing resentment. It is said that a successful diplomat improves its country's relations with another country even if the policy is unfriendly. Similarly, a bad diplomat worsens the relations, which is supposed to be good. The French statesman, Charles Maurice Talleyrand - Perigord holds, " A diplomat who says "yes" means " maybe", a diplomat who says " maybe" means "no" , and a diplomat who says "no" is no diplomat." (Wikipedia)

C Brown and Kirsten Ainley aptly define Foreign Policy by comparing it with domestic policy on the basis of two theories- Conventional International Relations theory and Realist theory. They state," Conventional International Relations theory, which assumes that the state is involved constantly in attempts at intervening in both environments, internal and external; that is, it engages in both 'domestic' and 'foreign' policy. Realist theory, as distinct from, for example, pluralism, assumes that these two forms of policy are different;in the case of domestic policy, the state is, in principle, capable of getting its way once having decided on a course of action; that is, it possesses both the authority to act, and the means to do so. In foreign policy, this is not so; outcomes are the products of interdependent decision-making. The state cannot expect that other states will respect its authority, because in an anarchical system, no state possesses authority, and whether the state has the means to get its way or not is a contingent matter-" (4)

They further elaborate the nature of diplomacy which they call 'statecraft' as well. "From foreign-policy perspective, states attempt to change their environment in accordance with aims and objectives they have set for themselves. From a structural perspective, states attempt to adapt to their environment,making the best of the cards the system has dealt them. Either way, states are agents; they act in the world." (5)

I am neither a career diplomat nor a student of political science. However, I have tried to tie up my thoughts on the subject, which are based on historical facts. My approach, which has been cast through my education, has made me objective and my bringing up in a region known as Madhes, which is the meeting point of India and Nepal, have shaped my thoughts. I have been expressing my views on India's role in Nepal through my occasional writings in newspapers and also on political development in Nepal and India.

The article of Prof. SD Muni, which was published in the book 'Nepal in Transition: From People's War to Fragile Peace' drew my attention. The book was much talked about some time back, as he had claimed that the then CPN-Maoist leaders, Pushpa Kamal Dahal 'Prachanda' and Dr. Baburam Bhattarai, had committed in black and white to the PMO of India in June 2002 for their cooperation and non-opposition to India in dealing with Nepal's affairs. They had also convinced the intelligence agencies of India.

Apart from it, interestingly, it was believed that India interfered in Nepal's internal matter in 2009 when the then UCPN-Maoist PM PK Dahal tried to dismiss the then CoAS Katwal. Later on, it was confirmed by Shyam Saran, the then foreign Secretary of India while interacting with the media during the launching of the book on 27 July, 2012. It is difficult to say whether India did really pressurize president Dr. Ram Baran Yadav directly or pressurized him indirectly by the memorandum submitted by the 22 parties to this effect. Was it an effective diplomacy of India in a limited time frame or a case of an Indian diplomat simply boasting it?

These two contexts were the immediate cause of my writings which were published in the Nepalese media since then. I have tried to put before the readers in brief the Nepal-India relations to ascertain the role of diplomacy. My regular interest in Indian and Nepalese political happenings, and my long stay in India in course of my studies, helped me develop a taste for writing on Nepal-India relations. I derive pleasure in writing on these subjects after interacting with the people who have fascination for criticizing India presuming its involvement in every vital decision of the government of Nepal.

The objective of the book is to enlighten the readers, especially from India with interest in India-Nepal relations on the one hand and draw the attention of those who formulate the Indian foreign policy towards Nepal and manage it diplomatically , on the other, to orient it for the future. The book is a study of the events that took place basically from 1951 and onwards to the present day Indian diplomatic activities in Kathmandu. To make readers and researchers understand Nepal's present internal and external complexities, some important historical events of the last two hundred and fifty years, have been discussed briefly.

This book has been divided into ten chapters. The first deals with overview of Nepal-India relations. The second chapter is related to Nepal's relations to India vis-à-vis China. The third chapter throws light on the psychological barriers affecting the relations. The fourth chapter deals with Nehru's personal diplomacy. The fifth deals with Post- Nehru Diplomacy. The sixth is related to Dr. Manmohan Singh's indirect diplomacy. The seventh is concerned with Narendra Modi's direct diplomacy. The eight is related to Counter Diplomacy. The ninth deals with Formal Diplomacy carried out by the Indian diplomats in Nepal. And the last derives the conclusions.

I am grateful to Leo E. Rose for I have based my narratives of the Nepalese history mainly on the basis of his book, "Nepal Strategy for Survival", especially while covering the political and diplomatic activities from 1768 to 1950, which are needed to enlighten the reader with the short history of Nepal. I have failed to obtain adequate information about the role of some ambassadors, for which I owe an apology to them. Before coming down to Indian diplomacy in Nepal, it is imperative to go in detail about Nepal and India relations, which will pave the way for critical study on this complex issue.

I am thankful to Daman Nath Dhungana, former Speaker, Nilamber Acharya, Nepalese ambassador to India, and Prof. Lok Raj Baral, former Nepalese ambassador to India for their valuable suggestions. I will be failing in my duty if I do not thank Er. Ganesh Khaniya for taking trouble in going through the manuscript of the book and correcting errors. I also thank Youbaraj Acharya, executive director of NTTP Institute, Kathmandu for making me available the information I needed from different websites from time to time for this book. I am also thankful to Akhil Sharma, Adroit publishers for printing the book. I thank all those who have helped me in course of writing of this book.

There are some mistakes, which remain uncorrected. I humbly crave the indulgence of the readers for the same.

Birendra Prasad Mishra.
92/22, Miteri Marg, Old Baneshwar,
11 June, 2019 Kathmandu, Nepal.

References:

1. Foreword written from Hong Kong on 14th April2010 for Mandala Reprint Edition of 'Nepal Strategy for Survival' written by Leo E. Rose, p-ix.
2. Khanal Yadunath, Essays in Nepal's Foreign Affairs, 1998, p,26.
3. Pradhan Bishwa, Behaviour of Nepalese Foreign Policy, 1996, p, 55.
4. Brown C, Ainly Kirsten, pp76-77.
5. Ibid. p-90

Contents

	Acknowledgements	*vii*
	Preface	*ix*
1.	Multifaceted Nepal-India Relations	1
2.	Historical Perspective of Nepal	8
3.	Psychological Barriers	39
4.	Indian Diplomacy- (1947-64)	71
5.	Post-Nehru Diplomacy	90
6.	Dr. Manmohan Singh's Indirect Diplomacy (2004-14)	101
7.	PM Narendra Modi's Hegemonic Diplomacy	110
8.	Counter Diplomacy of China and Pakistan	148
9.	The Formal Diplomacy:	161
10.	Conclusions:	173
	Bibliography:	*182*
	Appendix-1	*184*
	Appendix-2	*192*
	Appendix-3	*198*
	Apendix-4	*202*
	Annexure I	*206*
	Annexure II	*209*
	Annexure III	*210*

Chapter 1

Multifaceted Nepal-India Relations

Background:

Nepal: as per National Population and Housing Census Report 2011, is a country that houses 126 caste/ethnic groups with 123 mother tongues. There are ten religions. The census report indicates three geographic regions. Out of total population,

(1) Tarai constitutes 50.27 percent of the total population while
(2) Hill constitutes 43 percent and -
(3) Mountain constitutes 6.73 percent.

Important Chronicle Data:

Significantly, Nepal has acquired its present geographic size in late 18th century by the military activism of the Gorkha Raja (King) Prithvi Narayan Shah to expand the boundaries of his principality. He conquered other principalities and finally succeeded in capturing Kathmandu valley, known then as the valley of Nepal. King Prithvi Narayan Shah converted Kathmandu valley as the capital of Nepal. The kingdom was ruled, except 104 years by the Rana Oligarchy (1847-1951), by the Shah dynasty till it was finally abolished by the duly elected Constituent Assembly in 2008. The Constituent Assembly-2 passed the new constitution on 20 September, 2015 and elected governments have been formed at Central, Provincial and Local levels in 2017-8 .

Specific Relations Between India and Nepal

In South Asia, the relations between Nepal and India are unique and delicate, yet at times, these are defined and determined at diplomatic level alone as being done usually between two countries. In reality, it is of an existential nature, as the relations between any two neighbouring countries are the relations between two peoples more than the relations between two nation-states. The people settled on both sides of the international borders are of the same ethnic group. They have been living there for centuries irrespective of the fact that borders have been shifting with the political change of the areas, time to time. Moreover, there is no restriction of the movements of the people as the international borders are open. Every now and then, the relations between the two countries seem to be the relations of love and hate. This is the reason that the topic has not only been a subject matter of discussion and deliberation in political circles and among the intelligentsia but also among the common people of both countries.

Nepal: A Buffer State

Historically, in South Asia, the relations between the two countries acquired strategic importance after Tibet became the autonomous region of China making Nepal as the buffer state between India and China, which changed the geopolitics of Nepal. It was never under British India. But the first British resident was sent to Kathmandu in April 1802. However, the formal diplomatic relation was established through the 1815 Treaty of Sugauli. The Nepalese establishments had to deal with the British before 1947 in accordance with the treaties of 1792, 1801, 1815, 1860, and 1923. The 1815 Treaty of Sugauli reduced the boundaries of Nepal but the Treaty of 1860 extended it as a prize for helping the British army in capturing Lucknow, the capital of Avadha. After independence, both countries signed the Treaty of Peace and Friendship in September, 1950.

Complexity of Relations:

Perhaps, the complexity of relations is due to Nepal's' multi-facetedness of relations with India that have social, cultural, religious, economic, political, strategic, and individual overtones. Interestingly, several segments of society consider it differently. Politicians view it in one way when in power and reverse it when they are out. Similarly, diplomats, the ruling elite, and the common people too perceive it differently. Kathmandu, which continues to decide all policies, differs in its view from that of the people, who are settled on the international boarders. Hence, often it is questioned as whether these divergent views suggest that the relations between the two countries are subjective due to the varied interests of perceivers or these have any objectivity too. The Nepal-India relations have been defined and viewed from various perspectives in the past. There are several factors, which have influenced the relations between the two countries. These factors are:

1. Nature:

The first and foremost perspective is based on Nature. It is more realistic and comprehensive as well. The word, 'nature' has been used in two senses. First, as nature creates every thing, and second, as a characteristic or quality, which embedded to the very nature of a thing. First, Nature, as an external factor, played a vital role in defining the relations between the two countries. Secondly, nature as an internal factor, defines the relations on the basis of human (natural) relations, not on any externality or artificiality. There is one more perspective known as diplomatic/ political perspective or the relations determined by two independent nations defining their mutual relations.

The role of nature in human life as well as in the life of a nation is, at times, very significant. On the effectiveness of nature in human life, J. Bentham, in his book "Principles of Morals and Legislation" writes:-

"Nature has placed the mankind under two sovereign masters-pleasure and pain." He takes pleasure as the psychological basis of his gross altruistic hedonism or Utilitarianism. Similarly, in the context of Nepal-India relations, it will be appropriate to hold that Nature has placed the relations between the two nations under one sovereign master –the Himalayas. (1) The Himalayas determined the relation between Nepal and India, millions of years ago when a vast mass of land (the Indian tectonic plate) collided with the Asian mass or the Tibetan plate that gave rise to the lofty Himalayas. Since then, rivers started flowing towards the Indian Ocean and Arabian Sea through the southern slopes over which humankind had no say. Human life evolved much later. People settled on the banks of the rivers flowing through this area. And in course of time, human civilization started growing. The concept of political boundaries came only with the growth of civilization when the notion of the state came into being. These are human creations. In this way, in our part of the continent, the people were settled there before they were getting divided historically into states from time to time.

2. Human Bond

It is a historical fact that the primitive men and women wandered from place to place in search of better food and shelters as animals did for better pastures. Human civilizations had flourished on the banks of rivers where plenty of water for drinking and navigation for trade was easily available. Even plants extend their roots and branches for getting water and the sunrays for their survival and growth. Naturally, people prefer to lead easy life to hardships. People were settled in the area before they were politically divided into two states. In the Indian subcontinent, people have been migrating to different locations either in search of livelihood or to save their lives from invaders. In this context, it is accepted that people migrated towards north and east from west, as there was series of evasions from the western border to the region. Perhaps, it was a time, when there was no country like Nepal or India and there were no well-demarcated boundaries between these two countries, as they finally exist today after signing of the Treaty of Sugauli in 1815. Before the treaty, the Gorkha king Prithvi Narayan Shah and his successors had extended the borders in both east and west of Nepal in late eighteenth century. Of course, there were slight changes in the boundaries after 1857. The Treaty demarcated the international boundaries by 10-yard no-man's land (dashgaja). In this connection, Leo E. Rose writes, "For at least two millennia, the hill areas to the south of the Himalayas have offered shelter to waves of migrants, and the process continues, as the recent wave of Tibetan refugees escaping Chinese rules testifies."(2)

3. Cultural Affinity:

Apart from social relations, the cultural affinity and religious cohesion tied the relationship stronger. The people of the adjoining areas of Bihar and Uttar Pradesh hardly find themselves as foreigners when they visit Nepal and vice versa. Their daily market, water for irrigation and schools for education have brought them very close to attach importance to any formal or diplomatic relations.

The word 'Culture' stands for customs and beliefs, art, way of life and social organization of a particular group or country. The people living on both sides of the international border in particular have common culture. Their food habit, clothing and living patterns are same as these are the effect of the common climate. They have marital relations for a long time and the open border dispensation has facilitated the continued social relationship. They share the common local languages and have Hindi as common link language.

4. Religious Homogeneity:

In Nepal, there are mainly ten religions, to which the people of Nepal adhered. These religions are common in India. People of one country have their relations in another based on their castes and creeds. Indians visit the famous religious places in Nepal with pure adoration and the Nepalese people regularly go on pilgrimages in India. To name a few - 'Pasupatinath, Muktinath, Lumbini, and Janakpur etc. in Nepal and Kasi, Prayag, Bodha Gaya, Badri-Kedar, Amarnath, Rameshwaram and Puri etc. in India. The Hindus and the Buddhists intend to visit their respective religious places at least once in lifetime. The religious homogeneity is a strong binding force of the peoples of these two countries.

5. Personal Interest:

Citizens of one country are working in another's country. Their working establishes cordial relations between the peoples of the two countries. It is an extra bond of relations between them. Nepalese citizens working in the Indian army and in other fields establish strong bonds between Nepal and India. Similarly, Indians, who are working in Nepal, provide space for good relationship between the two countries.

6. State to State Relations/ Diplomatic Relations:

There is yet another perspective to look at Nepal-India relations. Since these two countries are sovereign, their relations are supposed to be determined as per the international norms. And at times, the diplomacy plays a vital role in directing the relations. Diplomacy ordinarily means management of a country's affairs by its agents abroad as per the direction by the Ministry of Foreign Affairs at home. Foreign policy of a country is supposed to be the extension of its domestic policy. To understand diplomacy, it is essential to go through the short history of Nepal, which covers the past relations of Nepal with its neighbours, and its present status with futuristic course.

References:

1. Mishra, Birendra Prasad, art. The Natural Nepal-India Relation' pub in The Free market (Khula Bazar) A Collection of Articles, August-September, 2010, Kathmandu.,
2. Rose, Leo E., 'Nepal Strategy for Survival', p.7.

Chapter 2

Historical Perspective of Nepal

Modern Nepal and its Interests vis-à-vis India and China:

Nepal's relations with India cannot be visualized through the prism of their bilateral relations. In order to have an objective view and an insight into the Nepalese mindset, a short historical account of the making of Modern Nepal and its political development have to be considered historically. It is, therefore, imperative to perceive events and political development in the background of China, as its existence and its concerns are significant in the development of Nepalese foreign policy.

The triangular relations have been discussed under three heads:

1. During 1769 to 1846,
2. During 1846 to 1947.
3. After 1947 and onwards.

1. The Relations during 1769 to 1946

In the second half of the 18th century, the Indian sub-continent witnessed two military powers emerging with insatiable desire to conquer territories to expand their territorial boundaries and trade. One, the East India Company with headquarters at Calcutta, which came from Britain to India for trade and commerce, wanted to have political powers to perpetuate its control over the land; it acquired and succeeded gradually in conquering the province of Bengal and Moghul Empire of Delhi, which was crumbling. It wanted to have unlimited control over the north India including the plain terrains of the southern slope of the Himalayas. Side by side, in the mountain region of the Himalayas; another military power led by the ambitious king Prithvi Narayan Shah of the principality of Gorkha, though small in size and capacity, came out with his military might and strategic acumen to expand the boundaries of the kingdom by conquering other neighbouring principalities. His strategy was to expand his territory to the east as far as possible and upto Kashmir valley in the west and to the Gangetic plains in the south. In the words of Leo E. Rose:-

"At the time of Nepal's greatest period of expansion (1770-1814), a favourite Nepali slogan was: "We shall wash the blood from our kukris in the Ganges," signifies the aim of the Gorkha rulers of the country to extend their sway over this (Terai land) valuable lowland region, which was then in a transitional stage as a result of the disintegration of the Moghul Empire in India. The British preempted Nepal in the area, however, and Kathmandu ended up eventually controlling only a narrow strip of territory, averaging10 miles in width, below the foothills" (1)

Capital Shifted to Kathmandu:

Prithvi Narayan Shah, after establishing his authority over Kathmandu valley in 1769, which was called Nepal, then, shifted his capital to Kathmandu from Gorkha with a stopover in Nuwakot. He visualized it as a "yam between two boulders" or "a root between two stones." (2). The King was staunch anti-British. However, he wanted to continue friendship with them to prevent the entry of British traders to Kathmandu valley. As a matter of fact, he used to manage all military supplies from India and did not antagonize the

British East India Company, till it obstructed the commercial route between Tibet, India and Kathmandu Valley, which used to be the transit point between India and Tibet.

Goal to Capture' Kantipur:

To conquer Kantipur, the main of the three principalities in Kathmandu valley, he started pressurizing its king (Raja) Jaya Prakash Malla. He obstructed the route of Nuwakot and Kerung. Since there was another route of Kuti for trade, the trade between India, Kathmandu and Tibet continued undisrupted.

Route Interrupted:

However, when Shah obstructed this route too, there was intervention by the East India Company (the British establishment in Betia, India) through sending Kinloch in support of Malla in 1767 on getting approached by the Malla ruler. But the Company did not succeed. Ultimately, Shah conquered Kantipur in 1768 and had control over the entire valley by 1769. Leo E. Rose writes in this connection,

"The failed expedition of Kinlock had succeeded in seizing some territory, which was restored to the Gorkha Raja after he agreed to pay an annual rent of 30 elephants to the Company. In 1776, the British recognized Gorkha's authority in the eastern Terai district of Morang, which had been conquered two years earlier by the Gorkhalis. In 1783, a British boundary commissioner decided in favor of the Nepali government in a dispute between Gorkha and an Indian zamindar, Mirza Abdulla, over Rautahat and Pachrauti districts. After 1786, the British stopped collecting duties on goods imported from Nepal. Although there were several border disputes, that grew out of the expansion of both powers into the area at the foot of the hills, the 1792 commercial treaty between Nepal and the Company was concluded."(3)

Premature death of Prithvi Narayana Shah:

After conquering Kathmandu, Shah passed away prematurely without stabilizing the kingdom he had expanded, on the one hand and without fulfilling his dream of expanding the frontiers of his kingdom further, on the other. After his demise, his son Pratap Singh Shah ruled for only 2 years and ten months as he died of malaria. He maintained the flow of trade with India and China. There was no tension with the British India as British Company was engaged in fighting with the insurgency of Mysore and Maratha states.

Subsequent Rulers:

Pratap Singh Shah's younger brother, prince Bahadur Shah, capable and trained under his father, assisted him for some time. Unfortunately, the king lost faith in him. He was arrested and banished to India. However, the sudden demise of the king at the age of 26, left his two and half-years old son, Ran Bahadur Shah to succeed his throne.

Rajendra Laxmi, Regent Queen:

His mother Rajendra Laxmi became the Regent to rule on his behalf. She got Bahadur Shah back to Kathmandu to assist her. He was again arrested due to suspicion of treason of eying the throne but was released subsequently. He retaliated and got the Regent Rajendra Laxmi imprisoned in the palace and started ruling and expanding the frontiers of kingdom. In course of his campaign often, he was out of the capital. So, in his absence, the Regent again restored her power and Bahadur Shah exiled himself to Betia (India) again. Regent Queen died of Tuberculosis in 1785 that made room for the emergence of Bahadur Shah as the Regent in her place again.

Achievements of Bahadur Shah as Ruler:

Regent Bahadur Shah invited war with Tibet that lasted for long, as he wanted to be in the father's shoes. He was eager to restore trade with Tibet, especially the use of Nepalese coin there, which was stopped by his father, who had obstructed the trade earlier. He waged war to belittle his adversaries in the palace, and also to establish his bravery. He was, however, forced to sign 1792 treaty with China and also with the British Company allowing finally the representative of the Company to visit Nepal. It also facilitated Indian interference in Kathmandu by Kadir Khan, Knox, and Kirkpatrick, which added complexities in the statecraft. Later, he was arrested for writing China twice seeking its assistance and killed in 1797 on the charges of unaccounted expenditure on the war.

Prithvi Narayan Shah and Bahadur Shah

There were similarities between the father and the son, as like his father, he expanded the kingdom, was suspicious against India and had faith and respect for China. In contrast, the former never sought any Chinese support, as he did not have direct confrontation with the Company but the latter approached China twice for its support against India and also for getting power from the clutches of his incompetent nephew and his coterie. As a result, he was jailed and killed for seeking support from China.

British Perception of Nepal:

Nepal was always scared of the British and the British took Nepal as an obstacle in having control over the entire north of India. However, owing to the second Nepal-Tibet war of 1791 in which Nepalese army was pushed deep into Nepal by the invading Tibetan army, forced Nepal to have a commercial treaty in1792. Regent Bahadur Shah signed the treaty for Rana Bahadur Shah's name. In mid-August1792, the Regent appealed the Company for, "ten guns together with ammunition, and ten young European versed in the management of artillery. Approximately, two weeks later, another letter was sent to Calcutta, this time requesting that British troops be sent to Nepal's assistance," (4) Significantly, British representative Abdul Kadir Khan was allowed to visit Kathmandu to negotiate with the palace. However, before another representative William J. Kirkpatrick visited Nepal in 1793, the deal with the Chinese was already completed.

British Commercial Mission:

Rana Bahadur Shah, who assumed power himself in 1794, dismissed the Regent subsequently. The British did not take the scrapping of the 1792 treaty of commerce kindly and held it as the first casualty of the dismissal. Governor-General, John Shore dispatched a commercial mission under the leadership of Maulvi, Abdul Kadir Khan with a view to testing the sentiment of Kathmandu. Ran Bahadur Shah, who was reluctant to receive the commission, delayed the visit that returned to India in March, 1796 without much success.

Changed Circumstances:

Internally, the powerful faction of Bahadur Shah, which was led by Damodar Pande, opposed the decision of Rana Bahadur Shah to choose his infant son Girvan Juddha (almost one and half years old) by a Brahmin wife, as his successor in 1798. After facing the opposition, he abdicated the throne and retired to a life of "religious meditation" in Kathmandu. His endeavour to reassert his authority again failed on account of the resistance by the Council dominated by Damodar Pande. Finally, he set out for Banaras in 1800 with his supporters, as military leaders were also not in his favour. At Banaras, he became active and started negotiation with the British for restoring his power at the cost of sharing land revenue with them. Ultimately, his negotiation forced the establishment of Kathmandu to sign the treaty of 1801 with the Company authorizing the posting of its representative in Kathmandu.

A Major Event:

Captain W. D. Knux, got posted after Rana Bahadur at Banaras, as a Resident to negotiate with Nepal in case of any dispute with the Company.

Treaty Dismissed by Wellesley:

However, the palace was against the stay of Knux, who returned to India in 1803 and subsequently, Governor-General Wellesley formally abrogated the treaty in 1804.

Later Incidents:

By 1804, with the drastic change in the power equation, Rana Bahadur returned to Kathmandu despite resistance from Damodar Pande and his faction. Pande was executed as per order of the Regent Rana Bahadur. The factional feud continued, which led to the assassination of Rana Bahadur in 1806. However, his close associate, Bhimsen Thapa controlled the situation by killing and executing dozens of people opposing him.

Actions Taken by Bhimsen Thapa as Ruler:

After securing his position, Bhimsen Thapa started expanding the western border upto Kashmir. He met resistance from Kangra King, who with military support from Ranjit Singh of Punjab stopped the march of Gorkhali army in 1809. Interestingly, Ranjit Singh was in favour of keeping Sutlaj as the boundary between Gorkhali occupied area and Punjab, which was not accepted by Kathmandu. Nepalese commander Amar Singh Thapa captured the territories of hill Rajas including those in plains in 1810, which antagonized the British.

British Suppression:

Thapa was instructed by the British not to extend his conquests to the districts below the hills. Since Nepal was not ready to confront the British without preparations, it accepted the British demands. In the mean time, Kathmandu intensified its diplomatic effort to get support from China. Its mission in Peking made yet another strong appeal for Chinese assistance in 1812 but again it was rejected through the usual evasive reply. Nepal unsuccessfully sought alliance with central Indian states like Holkers, Gwalior, Bharatpur, Rampur, Lucknow and Lahore. Ranjit Singh was the main stumbling block for Nepal.

British Troops Moved:

There was change of guard in India. Moria, who replaced Minto as Governor-General, wrote a letter to Kathmandu on 11 March, 1814 seeking Nepal's recognition of British jurisdiction in Sheoraj and Butwal within 25 days. Since Nepal did not reply on due date, British troops moved into both districts on 22 April, 1814 and secured control over there.

Defeat of the British Army:

Due to oncoming malarial season, the British detachments were withdrawn in May, Nepalese forces returned to reassert Kathmandu's authority there. Several Company officials were killed. As a result, in September 1814, British troops, which were divided into four columns, invaded Nepal. Troops led by General Morley, General Wood, General Gillespie and his successor Martindell suffered serous defeats. The fourth column led by General Ochterlony achieved success as after long fierce fighting, Amar Singh Thapa agreed at Malaun to the terms under which the Nepali Army retired with their arms and the territory between the Kali and Sutlaj rivers came under the control of the British.

Peace Negotiation Stopped:

After meeting diplomatic failures at both fronts- northern (China and Tibet) and at southern (some Indian states), Nepal tried its best to convince the British not to assert to another war unnecessarily and the British too found it difficult to wage another invasion in the hills. After peace negotiations, on 28 November, 1815 the Nepalese representative, Gujraj Misra signed an agreement with the British representative, Major Bradshaw, which Kathmandu refused to ratify, as Misra did not have plenipotentiary powers. It made the British to invade Nepal again. The invasion began in February1816 under Ochterlony. He was able to outflank the main Nepali defensive position at Makwanpur, which resulted in Kathmanu quickly dispatching Chandra Sekhur Upadhyaya to Ochterlony's camp with a copy of the Sugauli Treaty bearing the seal of the Maharaj.

Sugauli Treaty Accepted:

Ochterlony finally decided on 4 March, 1816 to accept Nepal's ratification of the Sugauli Treaty. The most important provisions of the Treaty -

(1) authorized the British to establish a Residency at Kathmandu,

(2) surrendered all of Nepal's hill territories west of the Kosi River as well as the disputed Tarai areas below the hills to the Company or its subordinate Indian states, and

(3) turned over the territories between the Singalila range and Tista river to the Company, which then restored to Sikkim(5).

China's Cold Shoulder Response:

Nepal sought help from China during the war. Even after the end of war, it wrote a letter to China seeking help against the Company, which was negatively replied by the General Sai-chung-a (Shee Chanchoon) the Chinese commander, who was deputed by the Emperor in May 1816 to lead an army to Lhasa to assess the situation there.

Another Letter from Nepal to China:

In response to the letter Nepal sent another letter on 10 June. 1816 seeking Chinese assistance to halt British expansion in defence of Tibet. Nepal sent a delegation, which reached Shigatse towards the end of September, was consisted of Dalbhunjana Pande, Ranbir Thapa and Bhakta Bir Thapa. The delegation had a letter from the king that sought blessing from the Emperor, relief and protection, as well.

Prolonged Rule of Bhimsen Thapa:

Bhimsen Thapa continued to rule as King Grivan Juddha died in November 1816 just after attaining his majority, leaving his two-year son, Rajendra Bikram Shah to succeed. Queen Tripura Sundri was retained as Regent extending support to Thapa. Even in his death, Thapa played diplomacy by seeking Chinese support while intimating the news of the death on 15 December, 1816. Failing to get any comment, he instructed the regular quinquennial mission to make personal appeal to the Emperor for assistance on 17 October 1818, which failed again.

Nepal's Foreign Policy Diverted:

Thapa was compelled to divert his foreign policy towards Company, as he failed to secure assistance from China. He sent Mathbar Singh, his most reliable supporter in 1834, as his emissary to Calcutta who returned empty handed. Moreover, with the death of the Regent in 1832, he lost his major support in the palace, which coincided with Rajendra Bikram's attainment of majority. Interestingly, Thapa delegated the management of foreign affairs to king Rajendra in 1833 himself.

Incidents After 1836:

In 1836, thapa was removed from his office and his family members were jailed on the alleged charge of poisoning of 6-month son of Rajendra. He attempted to commit suicide and died on 29 July 1839.

Significantly, King Rajendra too followed the path taken by Thapa. He sent Pushkar Shah on quinquennial mission on 14 July 1837 to Peking. In his letter to the Emperor of China, Rajendra described Bhimsen as a "pro-Feringhi Bhardar" and requested either troops or a subsidy of Rs.20 million to oppose the British. The mission met with stern refusal. During 1837-8, envoys were sent out to Nagpur, Banaras, Rewa, Hyderabad, Kuch Bihar, Mathura, Lahore, Kotah, Hardwar, Gwalior, Scindia, Bhutan, Burma, and Afghanistan. After getting disillusioned with establishment, British Resident Brian Hodgson threatened war if Durbar did not mend its ways, and Rajendra agreed to an engagement promising ceasing all intrigues by messengers and letters.(6)

Mukhtiyarship of Ranajung Pande:

After Bhimsen Thapa, Ranajung Pande was appointed Mukhtiyar on 8 February, 1840. The strained British-Chinese relations due to the first "Opium War" to impose opium trade upon China and the dispute at Canton inspired Durbar to appoint Ranajung Pande, who was most critical of the British. Two days later, a letter was written to China offering attack the British in India. The Amban did not send the letter to Peking informing Kathmandu that China was capable of handling the British force. Rajendra sent quinquennial mission under the leadership of Jagat Bam Pande in July 1842 with a letter to the Emperor asking for troops or financial assistance to cope with the alleged British threat to invade Nepal if it refused the transit of a British army to Tibet. Rajendra had proposed an exchange of the Tibetan district of Taklakot with its gold deposits for the vassal principality of Mustang in Nepal. Still another proposal was made by Jagat Bam to the Amban to have a dual Tibetan-Nepali administration of Kerung and Kuti under which Lhasa would administer these districts for ten years and Kathmandu for three years. By the time Jagat Bam reached Peking, the 'Opium War' had been settled and Nepal's request was rejected.

Pushkar Shah Made Mukhtiyar:

Pushkar Shah succeeded Ranajung Pande, who resigned on his own in 1840. Like Ranajung Pande, Pushkara Shah too was anti-British. Pushkar Shah failed in settling the claim of the British for collecting 18 village market tax in Parsa District, and the alleged charge against the king to speak against the British while addressing the armed forces, who had revolted against the planned abolition of salary in kind 'Tirja'. He was sacked as per the advice of the G-G Auckland shortening his tenure by hardly seven months. He was replaced by Fatya Jung Shah on 1 November, 1840.(7)

Role of Mathbar Singh Thapa as Prime Minister:

On the advice of queen Laxmidevi, king Rajendra appointed Mathbar Singh Thapa as prime Minster and C-in C on 26 December 1843. (8) He took revenge on his enemies. He pressurized the king and the queen to give state power to the prince Surendra Bikram on 25 November, 1844, who was under his influence. The other faction was in search of taking revenge on him and he was killed inside the palace on 17 May, 1845.

Conspiracies and Conflicts:

Due to the developed conflict of interest between the king and the Mukhtiyar Mathbar Singh Thapa, who were conspiring Rajendra's abdication in favour of his 14-year son, Surendra Bikram Shah, the king finally turned to Jung Bahadur Kunwar, Mathbar Singh's nephew, who supposedly cooperated in the assassination of the ambitious Mathbar Singh on 17 May, 1845. Since there had been frequent changes in the establishment, there was no significant departure in foreign policy. However, British Resident Hodgson played his role in the replacements of the Mukhtiyars.

Leo E. Rose rightly concludes,

"The period from 1837 to 1846, had been marked, then, by complete frustration for Nepal in the share of foreign policy'.

A Precise Sketch of Events:

In short, the characteristics of the period can be subsumed as follows:

a. Unfortunately, kings died prematurely and new kings enthroned were minors.

b. Mukhatiyars and mothers ruled indirectly by becoming the Regents of the kings.

c. It was a period when the boundary of Nepal was extended and lost to some extent.

d. The enmity between the Thapas and the Pandes for grabbing power eclipsed the role of royalty.

2. Relations during 1846 to 1947: Pro-British Foreign Policy:

The political events that took place between the ratification of the Treaty of Sugauli in 1816 and the shifting of real political power from the Shah dynasty to the Rana oligarchy in 1846 compelled Nepal to adopt its pro-British foreign policy. The domestic upheavals in the palace and its failure in obtaining support from China, on the one hand and from some Indian states, on the other, against the British, left Nepal with no alternative but to toeing the line of the British.

Condition After the Death of Mathbar Singh:

After the death of Mathbar Singh, there was almost political chaos as Pande family was eliminated from the political scene and the royal family was divided in factions. The killing of Gagan Singh, the Queen's principal supporter, on 14 September, 1846 gave a new turn. The Queen, in a state of fury, summoned all the important leaders to the Kot courtyard adjoining the Palace, where almost all rivals of Jung Bahadur were killed in course of leveling charges and counter charges. More than thirty officials lost their lives and many more were expelled from Nepal. On 16 September, 1846, King Rajendra appointed Jung Bahadur as Mukhtiyar, who gradually started redefining Nepal's relations with its neighbours.

First of all, he cancelled the quinquennial mission to Peking, which was scheduled to depart in 1847. However, after five years, he decided to renew the customary mission to Peking. It was sent in August, 1852 under the leadership of Gambir Singh. It reached Peking on schedule and was received with normal formalities and friendliness. Gambir Singh and his second in command both died in Peking and a junior officer Lt. Bhim Sen Rana became the leader. He was forced to follow an indirect route to Tibet and the commission returned back to Kathmandu on 22 May, 1854.

Jung Bahadur's War Against Tibet:

Against the backdrop of different international situations and out of his ambition to assume the throne after winning the war, Jung Bahadur launched a war against Tibet in 1855. British attention concentrated on war with Russia in the Crimea, the Chinese involvement a desperate struggle for survival against the Taiping rebels, death of the Sixth Panchen Lama and the eleventh Dalai Lama still a minor, Regent at Lhasa Yeshi G. Rating a weak personality, strained relations between the Dalai Lama's officials and Kashag, Tibetan hope to get remaining vestiges of Chinese authority eliminated added fuel to the fire of his decision. Before waging war, he advanced several reasons for dispute with Tibet.

Modified Treaty Ratified:

After repeated negotiations and personal consultations with Tibetan officials and the Chinese representatives with disruptions, the draft treaty was suitably modified for the approval of the Amban, and the four Kalons of the Kashag in 1856. On 31 July,1856, the Treaty of Thapathali was finally ratified.

A Crisis in Nepal-Tibet Relations:

Nepal-Tibet relations once again underwent a crisis in 1872 when Kathmandu accused Lhasa of permitting the maltreatment of Nepalese merchants residing in Tibet. A partial mobilization of the Nepali militia was ordered in January and the Nepali Vakil (lawyer) was withdrawn in 1873. The situation improved by 1875.

However, in 1883, armed hostilities became imminent with regard to a dispute between a Newari merchant at Lhasa and two Tibetan women over a piece of coral led.

This resulted in the destruction and plundering of 84 Nepali-owned shops by a mob led by monks from Drepung, Sera and Galdan monasteries. Some indirect role of the Tibatan authority was suspected as nothing was done to prevent the riot. Kathmandu, which was careful about Lhasa absolving itself from its responsibility for the riot, started another war preparation on large scale.

Negotiations for Peaceful Settlement of Dispute:

Due to internal conflict in the palace and the demise of Jung Bahadur in 1877, war was avoided and the palace arranged a peaceful settlement of the dispute. The Nepali Vakil, eighty Nepali merchants, the Tibetan commissioners and two Chinese officials set out for Kerung in January1884 to meet a Nepali delegation headed by Col. Tej Bahadur Rana and Kaji Laxmi Bhakta Upadhyaya. Negotiations started and after several weeks of negotiations, the two delegations signed a four-point agreement on 26 May, 1884. Tibet agreed to pay:

(a) Rs.942,098 as compensation,

(b) restore the plundered property,

(c) punish the looters and

(d) refer the involvement of Khampas to the Chinese Emperor for punishment.

Recruitment of Gorkhalis in the British Army:

Jung Bahadur, after becoming Prime Minster and Commander-in-Chief with the title of Sri Sri Sri Maharajah (Sri-3) by king Surendra on 28 June, 1857, consolidated his power by playing off the prince against the king and his queens. He brought his status equal to the king by becoming king of Kaski and Lamjung and established martial relations with the royal family. After securing his position internally, he diverted his attention to have good relations with the British anew assuming that China would not challenge his authority in the near future.

Incidentally, he got the opportunity to develop good relations with the British offering military support in suppressing the mutiny of the British Indian regiment in Meerut, which spread over many barracks in India against the British rule'.

The British Approach:

Jung Bahadur's offer was not acceptable to the British as mutiny was suppressed. However, military aid was needed by the British to crush Oudh(Abadha), which had become the centre of rebel activity.

On 10 December, 1857, Jung Bahadur led 8,000 Nepali troops. The army performed creditably in the fighting which culminated in the capture and looting of Lucknow that put Gurkhas to their considerable advantage.

Changed Approach of Jung Bahadur:

Jung Bahadur then met G-G Canning at Allahabad and sought his help to acquire the throne of Nepal. The wish was not fulfilled but he got back some parts of the tarai land, which Nepal had lost in 1814 war. He got back four current districts of the western region of Nepal. Since he was not fully satisfied, he put restrictions on Gurkha recruitment in British army, demanded recall of the Resident and gave shelter to Nana Sahib and Begam Hajarat Mahal of Nabab of Abadha.

Death of Jung Bahadur:

With the sudden demise of Jung Bahadur, family rivalry between 'Shamasher, (Brothers of Jung Bahadur') and 'Jung', (direct descendents or sons of Jung Bahadur,) took the centre stage of power and Ranodip Singh succeeded Jung Bahadur as Prime Minister. Sensing the situation, British Resident requested him to help the procurement of 1,000 'Volunteers' for Gurkha battalions as a token of his real friendship. The right of the British to recruit Gorkhas in the British army and the status of Nepal under the British rule seemed to dominate the British-Nepal relations. The British were always eager to get the restriction on recruitment lifted.

Recruitment of Volunteers:

After the assassination of Ranodip Singh on 22 November, 1885; Bir Shamsher became prime minister on 23 November. The British, knowing his weak position politically, gave him recognition within a week. He could not meet the British demand for direct recruitment but allowed servicemen in Gurkha units to visit their homes on leave to solicit volunteers. However, he permitted the Gurkha to go and take British service through his official order. He could collect about 500 volunteers who are mostly physically disqualified. By 1890, the recruitment problem for the Gurkha units had been largely solved.

Controversy over the Status of Sovereignty of Nepal:

Apprehending the support of Calcutta to the descendents of Jung Bahadur if a change of regime suited Calcutta, Bir Shamsher decided to strengthen relations with China and wrote near the end of 1885 to the Amban in Lhasa justifying the assassination of Ranodip Singh requesting the Emperor to bestow upon him with a title and an official uniform, which was accorded to him in August, 1889 by a Chinese envoy. He again wrote to China in 1886, seeking permission for the periodic mission to visit Peking and on receipt of the confirmation, the mission left Kathmandu in September 1886, which stayed in China and Tibet for nearly five years., probably to acquire information vital for Nepal and also to have direct relations with Peking. During the periodic dispute with Tibet, Bir Shamsher again wrote to the Amban in 1893 requesting permission to send a deputation to Peking. The delegation left for Peking in August, 1894 and returned in March 1901. Interestingly, the language of the letter was very submissive. It became controversial between Calcutta and Kathmandu, as Calcutta was interested in not keeping Kathmandu under the subjugation of China. However, it was clarified by Bir Shamsher, who died on 4 March,1901 in a mysterious condition.

British Suspicion About Nepal-China Relations:

Significantly, the British perception of Nepal started getting suspicious about Nepal's relations with China after 1886 mission. The Foreign Department Secretary, H.M. Durand, commented that the mission"undesirable" and that "sooner or later, we shall have trouble with China all along the Himalayas," but concluded that, "I am afraid we cannot help". (10) The then Resident Major E.L. Durand, who happed to be the Secretay's brother, "added to Calcutta's apprehension by his report of the reception given to the Chinese envoy who brought the patent of title for Bir Shamsher. The Resident charged that Chandra Shamsher, Bir's brother and second in line for succession, "always asserts openly that Nepal is subordinate to China, and is in no way so to the Government of India.". He concluded that, "the settled policy of the Darbar is to play off China against us, and to make use of a pretended subordination to that power as a safeguard against the spread of any influence over this country". (11) Durand's obvious approach further recommended, "the British should assert on Nepal. He argued that since the Foreign Secretary, who had earlier concluded that Nepal was, "in a position of quasi-subordination to us, if the Chinese really attempt to establish their influence in Nepal, we must object, and revise our relations with that state, not I think a very difficult matter with all Jung Bahadur's descendents under our protection"(12)

Deva Shamsher succeeded him but was not allowed to continue as Chandra Shamsher staged a successful coup d'etat on 26 June, 1901 forcing Deva Shamsher to resign. The British immediately recognized his authority. In 1901, the rivalry between Russia and British over Tibet became serious as a Tibetan delegation had visited Russia in 1900-01. Russian interest was challenged through Mongol Buddhist subjects in establishing contact with Lhasa. The mere hint of Russia's interest in Tibet caused worries in Calcutta.

Chandra Shamsher decided to get benefit from it by deriving certain advantages for himself and Nepal by playing a leading role to the 1903 Younghusband expedition to Tibet. The coronation Durbar at Delhi in January 1903 provided him with an opportunity to impress upon the Viceroy the necessity for taking prompt action in Tibet.

Sequence of Incidents:

On 1 October, 1903, the Younghusband mission, which had proceeded earlier to the Sikkim-Tibet border to conduct negotiation with Tibet, was authorized to cross the border. He finally occupied Lhasa on 3 August, 1904. Calcutta did accept the loan of several thousand yaks and porters for transportation. The Nepali Vakil was the single most important source of information on the attitudes of Tibetan authenticities. Chandra Shamsher tried to play a role of mediator supporting Calcutta. Before Lhasa was captured, the Dalai Lama fled to Mongolia, where he established direct contacts with Russian officials, which proved another headache for the British. At London's behest, the expeditionary force was withdrawn in 1905, and moved to reassure China.

Agreement Signed by London & China:

An agreement was signed on 27 April, 1906 by London and China committing not to annex any Tibetan territory and no interference in the internal administration of Tibet by London and not to permit any foreign state to interfere with the territory or internal administration of Tibet.

China's Changed Stance:

In view of the Chinese military campaign in eastern Tibet, Kathmandu sought permission for the periodic mission to proceed to China. Since China too was interested in improving relations with Kathmandu, China agreed immediately and the mission headed by Bharat Bahadur left Kathmandu in August 1906. Nepal was not serious about the Chinese forward move and obtained some benefits by way of getting modern arms from the British. China was eager to get Nepalese support in their campaign. Nepal expected some gain from a Chinese dominated Tibet. Kathmandu felt offended on the presumptuous Chinese claim to suzerainty over Nepal as Nepal used to address the Chinese Emperor very submissively. Although the Chinese rule of Tibet did not improve the conditions of the Nepalese traders and deprive the Nepali Vakil of his extraterritorial rights enjoyed by him, Chandra Shamsher wanted to extract some concessions from the British like, granting the rank of ambassador, deletion of the reference to Nepal as a 'Native State' and have a new treaty to recognize Nepal's independence. In return, its status was confirmed between independent Afghanistan and the 'feudatory States of India'. The 1911 revolution in China resulted in the abrupt expulsion of the Chinese from Tibet. Chandra Shamsher, again, tried to extract some advantages. He wanted to see Tibet as an independent state and prepared to help the Tibetan attain it. If China was given free hand in Tibet, Nepal would rectify its boundary with Tibet so that the political frontier might coincide in future with the natural boundary,i.e., the Bhairab Langur range in the Kuti-Kerung area.

Significant Role of Nepali Vakil:

Nepali Vakil had mediated the procedure of withdrawal of the Chinese force from the area. Significantly, doubts were cast on allowing Nepali missions to proceed to Peking on a regular basis in both Calcutta and Kathmandu even before the expulsion of the Chinese from Tibet. On the advice of the Amban in mid-1911 to send a Nepali mission to China next year, the British Resident informed Chandra Shamsher to take decision only in consultation with the government of India. The mission was first postponed and then cancelled, when Chandra Shamsher, on British advice; repudiated the Chinese interpretation of the significance of the mission and terminated the system resulted almost in the abrogation of diplomatic relations between Nepal and China.

Nepal's Independence Recognized:

Chandra Shamshesr was shrewd and he developed his personal relation with the Viceroy. He gave permission of recruitment to the British and helped the British during the first Word War in which more than 55,000 Gorkha soldiers were deployed. Another Trety Signed in 1923 He ultimately convinced the British to have another treaty that took place in 1923. After the victory in the first World War, Chandra Shamsher wanted back the land that Nepal had lost during 1814 war as a gift to Nepal but it was not considered and in its place he was granted Rs100,000 in his personal treasury.

Britisher's Strategy and Networking:

Chandra Shamsher was demanding independent status for Nepal. To his satisfaction and also of Nepali elite, the British brought changes in designation of the Resident to British Envoy and the Residency to Legation in June1920. He was, therefore, interested in having a new treaty, which was acceded to through the Friendship Treaty of 1923, signed on 21 December, 1923 at Sugauli. Nepal finally obtained an 'unequivocal' recognition of its independence. Article 2 of the treaty confirmed all previous Treaties, Agreements and Engagements, since and including the Treaty of Segowlie (Sugauli) of 1815, which have been concluded. The British Government further recognized Nepal's independence in 1934 when it agreed to the establishment of a Nepali Legation at London.

Chandra Shamshesr Allied with the British:

Chandra Shamsher, who died in November, 1929, had made the 'Alliance' with the British the basic theme in his foreign policy, even at the sacrifice of traditional Nepali goals. (13) Juddha Shamsher, who succeeded Chandra Shamsher, followed his predecessor during the Second World War by offering the loan of ten battalions of the Nepal state army for the use in India. The British also received permission to recruit 22 more Gurkha battalions for the British Indian army. In all, more than 200,000 Nepalis served in British units during the 2nd World War on the Burmese, Middle Eastern, and North African fronts.

Reasons for Setting Official Relations with the British:

The Ranas maintained official relations with British India, as they believed that the British would not leave India soon. They were having cordial relations with the Hindu Mahasabha, a Hindu Organization, which was supporting the Ranas as they ran the administration on Hindu pattern. However, when the interim government was formed in 1946, the Rana regime started to adjust itself with the new set-up. And the new Indian government too was willing to maintain its traditional relations. The two governments concluded a "standstill agreement" under which India's status as the successor power to the British was recognized and the terms of relationship between the two retained.

In the mean time, on 16 may, 1947, Padma Shamsher announced to have basic constitutional reforms. He proclaimed the constitution based on democratic line drafted by Indian Experts led by Sri Prakash Gupta on 26 January, 1948. The reform was not acceptable to a powerful faction led by C-in-C Mohan Shamsher who took over the reign. Keeping in view the Chinese forward policy towards Tibet and the democratic demands in the country, he signed the Treaty of Friendship with India on 31 July, 1950 to be discussed later in the book.

Demands for Democratic Rights:

However, the internal conflict of the Rana family seeking democratic rights and the political aspirations of the leaders seeking reforms living in Kathmandu and the Terai resorted to an armed revolution establishing parties outside Nepal rendering the collapse of the Rana oligarchy with the conclusion of the "Delhi Compromise" on 7 February, 1951 and after a lapse of 104 years, the Monarch reacquired his sovereign power to influence the politics of Nepal until monarchy was abolished by the elected Constituent Assembly in 2008.

The main features of incidents occurred during centuries above can be summarized here as under:

a. It was the period of effort to recover the lost land to British and strengthen friendly relations with the British.
b. During the period, the palace became weak and the centre of power was shifted from the hands of the king to Prime Ministers.
c. The transfer of power was made officially.
d. There was a clash of interests for succession as the role of succession was revised that led to assassination and mysterious deaths of Prime Ministers.
e. The familial rivalry made the political leadership weak compelling to accept the British interference.
f. This period can be categorized as period when Nepal was defining its political status and importance in the region.
g. In different contexts whenever Nepalese leadership was weak, the British tried their best to raise the question of recruitment and got benefited. Even during tensions with Tibet, the issue of recruitment was raised.

3. Relations after 1947 and Onwards:

After the end of Second World War, like India; which became independent in 1947- many other countries in different continents had started their democratic movements. Nepal too could not remain passive being cut off from the air of change blowing in several parts of the globe. India used to support independence movement in every country, as its leaders regarded independence as a birthright of every citizen. The independence movement in India gave impetus to the enlightened citizens of Nepal and also the young people living in the Indo-Nepal border area, who were either having their education in India or participated in the independence movement like "Quit India Movement."

After returning back from India, they too felt the necessity of freedom from the autocratic rule of the Ranas, and they formed their political outfits during 1947 to 1950 on Indian soil, as political activities were not allowed by the regime. On the other side, the regime too could not sit idle and keeping in view the mood of the people, the then Rana Prime Minister, Padma Shamsher JBR initiated the political reformation by framing a new constitution for the country and held elections.

Opposition to Oligarchic Rule of Ranas:

However, in Kathmandu, the resentment of the Nepalese people was brewing against the oligarchic rule of the Ranas. It was getting expressed in disguise by literary works and dramas. In Kathmandu, in the year 1940, some people were arrested and four revolutionaries were executed for raising their voices against the regime. People were silently opposing the Rana oligarchy, on the one hand, and on the other, in Terai, some youths, who had participated in the Indian independence movement, formed a political party in India, as political activities were banned. The party started its armed revolution to overthrow the rule. Side by side, the monarchy, which was sidelined by the Rana oligarchy for 104 years, silently, opposed the Ranas and took shelter in the India embassy, and finally shifted to Delhi in self-exile.

A Conclusive Effect:

All these factors led the establishment to negotiate the political settlement in Delhi. The negotiations took place there and a tripartite agreement in the form of 'Delhi Compromise' was reached. The Compromise restored the monarchy with a commitment to establish democratic setup in the country. And to implement the agreement, the sitting Rana Prime Minster was allowed to continue with a coalition government of the revolutionary Nepali Congress. The Ranas and the Nepali Congress participated in the government in equal numbers of ministers. Consequently, a new political era began in early 1951. The changed contexts of interests, thereafter, will be dealt with in course of the book.

The main features of this period are as here under:

1. The Second World War changed the scenario of the world politics,
2. Countries like India became independent, which inspired the people in Nepal to have democratic rule in the country.
3. Kathmandu took the lead by opposing the 104-year-Rana oligarchy in Nepal, which resulted in the execution of four revolutionaries by the regime.
4. The Nepali Congress started an armed revolution in the late 1950 against the regime.
5. The king facilitated the over through of the Rana regime by self-exiling himself to India that forced the ruler to negotiate with the king and the Nepali Congress.
6. India brokered the deal to have a peaceful political transition.
7. Monarchy was restored with the assurance of establish democracy through the election of the Constituent Assembly.

8. To implement the agreement, a coalition government under the sitting Rana PM with the Nepali Congress was formed.
9. People were enthuastic about the political transformation.
10. Democratic developments saw many ups and downs.

Indian Support:

India connotes three dispensations-pre-British period (1769 onwards), British period (1816 onwards) and post-British period or post-Independent India (1947 onwards). The previous historical perspective has shown some light on Indian support to Nepal. During pre-British period, for the first time, Ranjit Singh, the king of Punjab refused to support the Gorkhali army moving towards Kangra as his own interest was at stake. It suggests that Nepal under Amar Singh Thapa and Bhimsen Thapa sought Indian States' support to expand its territories. Bhimsen Thapa under the rule of minor Grivan Juddha and also under his minor son king Rajendra Bikram sought help from some Indian States against the British. Ran Bahadur Shah too sent letters to some Indian States seeking their support. Ran Bahadur was the first king of Shah dynasty to seek support from princely states of India against the British rule, which were themselves fighting for their independence against British subjugation.

Nepal, the British and Independent India:

During the Rana oligarchy, Rana Prime Minister never demanded any help except when China was heading towards Tibet. It succeeded in getting arm support from the British. Of course, some weak prime ministers sought recognition from the British. On the contrary; Nepal supported the British in 1857 and in both First and Second World Wars.

Even in post-British period, the Rana government provided military supports to India in its war against Pakistan and in Hyderabad Action in 1948 to annex Hyderabad state of Nizam. Of course Padma Shamsher sought Indian support in drafting its constitution in 1949 by way of constitutional expert. However, king Tribhuvan sought refuge in the Indian embassy to get rid of the Rana regime in 1950 and the results are known and discussed elsewhere.

Chinese/Tibetan support:

The founder of the Shah dynasty and creator of modern Nepal, Prithvi Narayan Shah was suspicious against British India and had faith and respect for China. He never sought any Chinese support, as he did not have direct confrontation with the Company. However, his second son Bahadur Shah approached twice for its support against British India and also for getting power from the clutches of his incompetent nephew and his coterie but he failed in his attempts.

China's Cold Shoulder to Nepal

To confront the British, Kathmandu under Bhimsen Thapa intensified its diplomatic effort to get support from China, as war with the British company was lurking round the clock. The Nepalese mission in Peking made yet another strong appeal for Chinese assistance in 1812 but again it was rejected through the usual evasive reply. During the war of 1814 and thereafter, Kathmandu wrote to China seeking help against the Company, which was negatively replied in May 1816. In response to the letter, Nepal sent another letter on 10 June, 1816 stressing the need of Chinese assistance to halt British expansion in defence of Tibet. It also sent a delegation with a letter from the king seeking blessing from the Emperor and relief as well as protection. Even in the death of Grivan

Juddha, Thapa played diplomacy by seeking Chinese support while intimating the news of the death on 15 December, 1816. Failing to get any comment, he instructed the regular quinquennial mission to make personal appeal to the Emperor for assistance on 17 October, 1818, which failed again. Consequently, Thapa was compelled to divert his foreign policy towards the Company.

King Rajendra's Approach Also Failed:

Significantly, King Rajendra sent Pushkar Shah on 14 July, 1837 to Peking to continue the quinquennial mission with a letter to the Emperor describing Bhimsen as a pro-British Mukhtiyar and asked for either troops or a subsidy of Rs.20 million to oppose the British. The mission failed to achieve its mission. There was a change of guard and Ranajang Pande was made Mukhatiyar. He, just two days after his appointment, wrote China through Amban in Lhasa offering attack the British in India. But Amban did not send the letter to Peking and informed Kathmandu about its capability of handling the British force. Rajendra did not stop there and continued his effort by sending quinquennial mission under the leadership of Jagat Bam Pande in July 1842 with a letter to the Emperor asking for troops or financial assistance to cope with the alleged British threat to invade Nepal if it refused the transit of a British army to Tibet. He went further by proposing an exchange of the Tibetan district of Taklakot with its gold deposits for the vassal principality of Mustang in Nepal. Still another proposal was made through Jagat Bam to the Amban to have a dual Tibetan-Nepali administration of Kerung and Kuti under which Lhasa would administer these districts for ten years and Kathmandu for three years. But all these requests were rejected.

In the early stage of Rana regime, Jung Bahadur did not approach China and Tibet for any support. Ranodip Singh followed suit. However his successor, Bir Shamsher wrote thrice during his tenure. Dev Shansher succeeded Bir Shamsher who died in a mysterious condition. But he was not allowed to continue as Chandra Shamsher had overthrown him in 1901. In view of the Chinese military campaign in eastern Tibet, Kathmandu, sought permission for the periodic mission to proceed to China. Since China too was interested in improving relations with Kathmandu, China agreed immediately and the mission headed by Bharat Bahadur left Kathmandu in August, 1906.

The 1911 revolution in China resulted in the abrupt expulsion of the Chinese from Tibet. Interestingly, Nepali Vakil played a significant role of mediating the procedure of withdrawal of the Chinese force from the area. Significantly, on the advice of the Amban in mid-1911 to Nepal to send a Nepali mission to China next year, the British Resident objected it and advised Chandra Shamsher to take decision only in consultation with the government of India. As per British advice, the mission was first postponed and then cancelled as he repudiated the Chinese interpretation of the significance of the mission. He finally terminated the system that led to a formal abrogation of diplomatic relations between Nepal and China.

References:

1. Rose, Leo E, Nepal Strategy for Survival, p-5,
2. Ibid., Preface, p. xiii, Nepal Strategy for Survival,
3. Ibid. p- 33-4.
4. Ibid. p- 68,
5. Ibid, p-89.
6. Ibid, p- 98-99
7. Acharya Baburam, Aba Yasto Kahilai nahosa, pp-72-74, 2055 BS).
8. Acharya, Yagyanath, Nepal ko Itihasa, p. 105
9. Rose, Leo E, pp-96-102)

10. Ibid. Rose p-144,
11. Ibid, p. 145
12. Ibid
13. Ibid. pp-170.

❖ ❖ ❖

3

Chapter

Psychological Barriers

Sometimes, multifacetedness misguides people to form a judgment. This has happened greatly in regard to Nepal-India relations, which are not only multifaceted but centuries-old too. Consequently, different perceptions are held by divergent sections of Nepalese society. Interestingly, politicians view it in one way when in power and reverse it when they are out. Similarly, diplomats, the ruling elite, and the common people too perceive it differently. Kathmandu, which still continues to decide all policies, differs in its view from that of the people settled on the boarders. Their common suffering and happiness, economic, religious, social mingling, day to day purchasing at local hat (Bazar), social feasting and the marital relation etc, can hardly be realized by the people living quite far off places like Kathmandu.

Interestingly, L.E. Rose referring to the unpublished manuscript of Bhuwan Lal Joshi stated:-

"The Psychological Basis of Nepali Attitudes to China and India,", quotes Joshi, "Nepali had to reckon with the Indians so long and so often that they are more prone to infer the latter's intents quickly than to observe their overt behavior. Due to the high degree of intimacy between the two countries through the ages, whatever the Indians do that in actual practice; is not considered as important as what the Nepalis think the Indians mean. With the Chinese, however, it is a different story." In this connection, he writes, "Indeed, a whole new historical mythos, recently formulated in Nepal, aims at providing that cultural and intellectual influences from China and India have been equally important in shaping Nepali social values and culture. Factually, this is nonsense, but psychologically it makes very good sense."(1)

There are the twists and turns in India-Nepal relations by way of psychological 'barriers' in their places.

In psychology, "barrier" stands for any obstruction in the process of looking at things or conditions and interference with achieving the needs and aspirations. Barriers are explained as more or less insurmountable obstacles. We perceive or conceive things objectively, yet at times we are forced to look at things in a different way under the influence of some psychological or mental and external conditions, such as, background or context and meaning, our past experience, socio-cultural inheritance, official positions, interests, habits, ideologies, identities and personal barriers including weakness, complexes, lack of skill, low intelligence, etc. Barriers also include internal tension, irritability.

Complex Perception of Nepal-India Relations:

It is not easy to perceive the relations existing between two neighbouring countries like a perception of an object directly. For example, viewers conceive our relations with India or China, differently. When we talk about our two immediate neighbours geographically, we call China as northern neighbour and India as southern neighbour, even though we know well that we are surrounded by India on east and west, too. We say so because China, a bigger and mightier country is on our north, in contrast, India, which is relatively smaller in size and weaker in military strength, is called only a southern neighbour. It is also viewed so because the lengths of eastern and western borders are lesser in size than those of northern and southern borders. Nepal sees itself surrounded by India on three sides, whereas India sees Nepal as a crucial frontier that exists between it and China.(2) Climatically, there are snow covered peaks and high mountains in the northern parts of the country to make the life of the people hard to live in comparison to that of the southern part where life is easy to live.

1. Perception of Nepal:

Nepal, in the present geographic size, is the creation of military power exercises to bring together small principalities in late 18th century by king Prithvi Narayan Shah of Gorkha principality and his successors. Subsequently, Kathmandu valley was made the capital of Nepal. Hitherto, Kathmandu valley was Nepal. It is evident from the narration by Colonel William J. Kirkpatrick, who visited Nepal in 1793, called the valley as 'the valley of Nepaul'(3) He was deputed by Marquis Cornwallis, G-G of the British India to mediate in the dispute between China and Nepal. Similarly, in 1905, Slyvian Levy, in his first volume of his book written in French language "Le Nepal", defines Nepal Valley under the heading 'Nepal Valley', in these words:-

"Nepal Valley (Nepal) is situated on the midway from the plains of India to the high peaks of the Himayas".(4) Earlier, Nepal was limited to the present Kathmandu valley itself. Curiously, even during the last 150 years, Kathmandu remained the capital of Nepal and was always called Nepal by virtue of its dominance in every aspect of life. This very contradiction in perception and reality influenced the relations between Nepal and India to a great extent.

2. Open Border Dispensation:

There are some major psychological barriers that irritate the relations, barring some secondary ones. Primarily, it is the government, dominated by the people who suffer from the Kathmandu dominance syndrome. The foremost barrier is the open border dispensation. The syndrome represents a mindset holding all Madheshis as emigrants from India and their continued influx causes demographic shift. Not with standing the data of the census reports of the last fifty years clearly proving the increased population in Tarai due to migration of the people from the hills in great number, it supports the mindset. It is also a fact that people from India have come and shettled in Nepal, especially in the southern side of the East-West Highway constructed about four decades ago mainly through the jungles of Tarai rigion. The region was hardly habitable due to Malaria and dense forest. The villages of tarai were already thickly populated earlier, of course with no communication system at all. The assertion that criminal activities in Nepal have their genesis in India, as criminals are active from there, is partially true because, it happens from both sides.

The issue of Open border dispensation between India and Nepal, which exists from time immemorial, is an issue being raised intermittently by Nepal, it was raised in the Panchyat regime with a view to controlling the political activities, guided by the political leaders residing in India, demanding political freedom taken away by the monarchy. In Panchayat era, especially, Dr. Harka Gurung, a renowned geographer came out vehemently against the so called large scale migration from India, perhaps, finding the similarity between the faces of Madhesis and Indians, on the one hand, and unfair data collected by him, on the other. He raised the issue of controlling/sealing the border on account of the high growth of population in Tarai region, due to migration of the people from India to this region. Regretfully, it is unthinkable as to how did a scholar like him too follow suit of the same old mindset ignoring the factual data furnished by every census report that the people of the hills had been migrating to the plains in large numbers? In this connection, Rishikesh Shaha writes:

"But if we look at Nepal's Census figures, it does not appear that there has been an alarming growth of immigrants from India into the Tarai. According to the 1981 Census figures, there has been a considerable shift of population from the Nepali hills. In 1971,62.39 percent of the population lived in the hills and only 37.61 percent in the Tarai, while in 1981 only 56.33 percent of the population was found living in the hills and 43.67 percent in the Tarai. There has been thus an increase in the Tarai population by 6 percent as a result of internal migration itself. According to the latest 1991 Census, 53 percent of the population are living in the hills and 47 percent in the Tarai. Again if we look at the 1981 Census figures for those who speak the more important Tarai languages of Indian origin, we do not find a normal increase in their ratio to the total population. In some cases there has been a decline in the numbers". (5)

Moreover, the process of migration from hills to plains was accelerated with the construction of the East-West Highway together with the policies of the government to settle as much people as possible from the hills to the plains to influence the domination of the local people politically and economically. The process of resettlement of landless people from hills to plains in the forest areas is still continuing. Recently, the Maoists arranged such settlement in Dhangarhi district and the government was resorted to firing killing some people to the save forest from deforestation and human settlements.

The Kathmandu ruling class including the monarchy has been opposing directly and indirectly the open border phenomenon. India was pressurized indirectly in the past to close its boarders with Nepal. In the 1960s, Chinese goods were imported enormously and smuggled to India for three purposes: first, to get Indian currency for its economy; secondly, to please China by importing its goods and thirdly, to force India to close its borders to safeguard its economy. Moreover, Nepal's seemingly insensitiveness towards terrorists, especially indirectly, convinces India of the uselessness of open border dispensation. Perhaps, the Nepalese reluctance to signing of extradition treaty may be another instrument to pressurize India on the issue.

Significantly, during the high pitch of insurgency, the insurgents were supposed to have taken shelters in India and got arms and training regularly due to being open border situation. The issue of open border situation got politicized, turning Nelson's eye from the fact showing photographs of long queues of young people waiting to register their names at the Indian check posts published in our national dailies. There were reports that the young people working at Mahendranagar (Kanchanpur) in daytime, used to take shelters at Banbasa (India) fearing from the insurgents who might recruit them forcefully. However, it is an annual regular routine for the poor people in western High Mountain to go to India to earn their livelihood in the winter season for trading every year and forced to go there when there is draught making life difficult to maintain.

A Latest Development:

Interestingly, the inability of the Emminent Persons Groups of India and Nepal to submit their joint report to the Indian PM Modi, has become the headlines of print media these days, as it is believed to have suggested some kind of border regulation, which is not fully acceptable to India. (The issue has been dealt with in detail in regard to the Treaty of 1950.)

3. The 1950 Treaty:

Another major psychological barrier of perception is the Treaty of Peace and Friendship (Appendix-1), which was signed on 31 July, 1950 by Chandreshwar Prasad Narayan Singh, Ambassador Extraordinary and Plenipotentiary of India to Nepal and Mohun Shamsher Jung Bahadur Rana, Maharaja, Prime Minister and Supreme Commander-in-Chief of Nepal.

The 1950 Treaty seems to be the modified version of the Treaty of Friendship (Appendix-2) signed by W.F. O'Connor, Lieutinent-Colonel, British Envoy at the Court of Nepal and Chandra Shumshere, Prime Minister and Marshal of Nepal on 21 December, 1923. It has seven Articles. It seeks perpetual peace and friendship and acknowledges respect for each other's independence. It confirms all Treaties, Agreements and Engagements including the Treaty of Segowlie. It commits preservation of peace and friendly relations with the neighbouring States whose territories adjoin their common frontiers to the mutual interests. It allows all measures to prevent its territories being used for purposes inimical to the security of the other. Nepal will be free to import from or through British India into Nepal whatever arms; ammunition, machinery, warlike material or stores may be required or desired for the strength welfare of Nepal. No custom duty shall be levied at British Indian Ports on goods imported on behalf of the Nepal government for immediate transport without breaking bulk en route of a rebate of the full duty paid. Rebate may be claimed on the basis of a certificate signed by an authority.

In contrast to the Treaty of Friendship of 1923, the 1950 Treaty was named 'Treaty of Peace and Friendship'. It has ten Articles containing matters related to political, diplomatic, security, and trade-commerce. It provides for - (i) continuity to the centuries-old free movement of citizens in each other's territory, (ii) right to participate in each other's development projects, (iii) privileges in the matter of residence, and (iv) ownership of property. (v) It acknowledges the sovereignty, territorial integrity and independence of each country. (vi) The two Governments have to inform each other of any serious friction or misunderstanding with neighbouring state likely to cause any breach in the friendly relations subsisting between the two governments.

Perhaps, the term 'state' used here and 'states' used in Article 3 of the 1923 Treaty are meant to denote 'states' of India and not independent states. It binds both countries to maintain normal diplomatic relations. It authorizes Nepal to import arms and ammunition from and through India. It cancels all previous treaties, and provides for termination of the treaty by any country by giving one year's notice.

Opposing Mindset of the Treaty:

Politicians, diplomats, and Kathmandu elite have been criticizing it, as a treaty between unequals. Maoists too had waged their war in early 1996 opposing this treaty along with other anti-Indian demands. Considering its implementation in totality, one may confront with the reality that several Articles, including Arts. 6 and 7 have been rendered ineffective gradually. Nepal deliberately scraped the idea of bringing Nepal under the defence-umbrella provided by India by getting the Indian wireless operators ousted from the posted at the Tibet borders in early 1960s. Armed vehicles and arms and ammunitions were imported from China and other countries. It nullified the letters exchanged between the government of India and the ambassador of Nepal on 30 January, 1965.

Legal Provisions for Making Treaty Ineffective:

Further more, no Indians are allowed to keep land and have industries without acquiring Nepalese citizenship. No bank account can be opened without citizenship certificate. No Indians are allowed to work permanently. No Indian companies are getting priorities over other countries in matters of contracts etc. making the Articles 6 and 7 ineffective, except the privilege of free movement of the people of one country to another. For centuries the border has been opened for the people who want to go on pilgrimage. Hundreds of poor and unemployed people from western hill visit India for earning bread and butter, and indeed, the Madhesis who have marital relations continue to remain in touch with their relatives in Bihar and Uttar Pradesh states in India for centuries. Over and above, thousands of common people visit across border local bazars to procure the materials they need to meet their day-today needs. Significantly, the government of Nepal employed school teachers, professors, medical doctors and engineers to meet the needs of the country. However, with the urbanization taking place, some semi-skilled workers from Tarai and adjoining border areas in India started coming to Kathmandu for work as there were heavy demands for carpenters, masons, plumbers, and labourers for construction of houses etc. which the local people could not meet. Along with them semi-skilled workers, some vegetable vendors and hawkers too landed in Kathmandu for purchasing empty bottles and waste papers and rag-pickers, perhaps, to keep Kathmandu clean and earn their bread and butter.

To have an insight into the Treaty, it has to be viewed from different angles. The agreement meant for the people of Nepal with the changed connotations. Interestingly, till 1959 (when the first elected government was formed), Kathmandu valley stood for Nepal for all practical purposes.

Visa for Kathmandu and Land Revenue in Indian Currency:

Till 1951, everybody, whether he belonged to Tarai or hills, had to acquire visa for entering Kathmandu. Till 1959, the land revenue in the entire country excluding Kathmandu was being collected in Indian currency in Tarai and other regions. Patha University used to conduct college examinations before Tribhuvan University came into existence in 1959.

Purpose of Treaty in Challenged:

Politically, the Treaty appears to be signed by the last Rana Prime Minster to save the oligarchic Rana-rule that was threatened with the active democratic forces on the one hand and with the rising communist China, on the other. But alas, he failed to perpetuate his rule in the complex context of democratization of the kingdom. It continued the traditional free movement of the citizens also to clear the dense forest of Tarai infested with malaria for resettlement and for financial benefits. During the Panchayat era, the kings were apprehensive about the activities of the pro-democratic elements residing in India. King Birendra's proposal for declaring Nepal a zone of peace was just to neutralize the Treaty. It was proved useless when India did not accept it; though more than hundred countries had accepted it.

Three Classes of People Benefited:

Interestingly, the treaty, which establishes special relations with India have benefited three classes of people, who still value it. (i) For instance several millions of hill origin people living in India for their livelihood and (ii) people living across the border (i.e. the Madhesi) having blood relation (through marital relations) for centuries. And thirdly, the people who have religious faith, both Hindus and Buddhists, have pilgrimage without any hustle for centuries.

Use of Treaty:

Of course, some segments of society and the government of Nepal did not take the treaty kindly, as some Maoists at the time of insurgency, and some armed groups were utilizing the dispensation permitted under the treaty. Before Maoist insurgency, the Nepali Congress started armed struggles twice against the government from the Indian soil had annoyed the then establishment. Some pseudo nationalists, especially from the Valley, had been constantly spearheading their voices against the treaty.

Formation of Eminent Persons Group (EPG):

There has been a constant demand in Kathmandu by some groups and political parties to change or reject the Treaty altogether. In this context, the governments of India and Nepal decided to form a group of eminent persons to review the Treaty and recommend their suggestions for modification in the changed contexts. During the first visit of Indian PM Modi' to Nepal, it was decided to form a group of four persons from each side to constitute the Eminent Parsons Group (EPG).

Small-Sized EPG:

The initiative of forming the EPG had taken place during the Prime ministership Dr. Manmohan Singh, when the then Nepalese PM Dr. Baburam Bhattatais visited India. During their meet, it was agreed upon to have a committee, but no such formation could take place. It was PM Modi who took up the thread during his last visit to materialize the agreement. It is intriguing as to how it remained unexecuted till the late PM Sushil Koirala's tenure ended. It was not known whether he didn't take the initiative in this regard or he failed in his endeavour to select the four eminent persons where PM Oli succeeded. Did other parties including the Madhesi outfits not accept Koirala's nominees? PM KP Sharma Oli formed the group during his earlier stint before visiting India. Significantly, Manmohan Adhikari raised for the first time the issue of the treaty during his visit to India as a PM in 1995, which was responded by his counterpart seeking his proposal and the issue lingered henceforth. The government formed EPG on 27 January, 2016 that consisted of Dr. Bhesh Bahadur Thapa (former ambassador to India and foreign minister), Neelamber Acharya (former minister, ambassador to Sri Lanka and the ambassador designate to India), Surya Nath

Upadhaya (Former bureaucrat) and Rajan Bhattarai (leader of the ruling CPN-UML, now CPN) for reviewing all existing bilateral agreements with India including the 1950 Peace and Friendship Treaty with the mandate to "review, up-to-date and adjust" as per the present context and strengthen further the existing relations between the two countries.

Views in Opposition:

Significantly, some were aghast at the formation, as to how the multifaceted relations between Nepal and India could be reviewed, and updated in a limited span of two years by four persons alone. To some, since the group represents only one community and represents the Kathmandu elite, its recommendations may not be acceptable to the Madhesis, the original inhabitants on the both sides of the international borders. The process of formation of the group smacks partisan and arbitrary. Curiously, some members are known for their public stands on the open border dispensation. Interestingly, PM Oli was learnt to have directed the GEP on Feb.2, 2016 not to repeat mistakes that had been committed by Nepal in the past and move ahead without compromising on national interests, as if Nepal had committed the mistake by signing treaties including the treaty of 1950 under review. (6)

Work Done by EPG:

India, too, promptly constituted its EPG. The group started its meetings. The first meeting was held in Kathmandu on July 4, 2016,with a provision for a two-year non-extendable term. The Group has already completed its task of preparing its report, which is likely to be submitted to the Indian PM Modi first and then to the Nepalese PM Oli.

A Note of Caution:

It is commonly apprehended that it may be used as a means to be played in the hands of a few politicians as its recommendations, if unrealistic, will be difficult to be implemented, on the one hand and it might land the country in another conflict apart from the existing one, on the other. Some skeptics hold that the vastness of the TOR of the EPG may lead to nowhere and it may prove to be a futile effort as the complex issues of cultural relations existing from the time immemorial can hardly be reviewed and adjusted in the 21st century, when borders are being made irrelevant day by day through - out the world and natural resources are being harnessed for serving the humanity.

4. Water Resources

The fourth barrier is related to the utilization of some common rivers and water resources. After India became independent, the top priority for the state and centre governments was to give immediate relief to the people of Eastern India who used to suffer hugely every year, without fail, due to floods. Hence, there were negotiations with the Government of Nepal to tame the big rivers, which flow through Nepal and cause serious flood effects in Bihar. Consequently, in 1950s, Koshi and Gandak projects were signed by India and Nepal.

Unkind Perception of Nepal:

Signing of these projects were largely criticized in Nepal as its water resources were harnessed in favour of India ignoring the interest of Nepal. Though, the Gandak project, which was signed later could address some of the grievances raised by the Nepalese side, it is commonly accepted that Nepal has been deceived by India in Koshi and Gandak river projects, as Nepal has been denied of its rightful share of the anticipated benefits. Really, these were flood-controlling projects. It is a truism that had there been no Koshi project, the economic transformation of the people of the eastern districts of Nepal would not have been uplifted soon or would have been delayed considerably. No doubt, by taming Koshi, the people of Bihar got rid of their enormous sufferings as Koshi was regarded as the "sorrow river". Comparatively, limited Nepalese areas are saved also from floods.

Perhaps, these projects were signed with a view to harness cooperation aiming at human welfare at large, sometimes, ignoring the borders as to which side was benefited more. It was for two reasons. Firstly, the then political leaders were equally concerned about the welfare of India and Nepal since they had their education in India and had also participated in Indian independent movement. Secondly, the rivers' flow is longer in India than Nepal. In the same way, thirdly, Nepal was not in a position to meet the expenses as it had been free from the oligarchic rule of the Ranas hardly a few years ago and it did not have sufficient financial resources to meet the costs of projects.

On the contrary, in view of the past experience, Nepal became reluctant to go for any project with India for further sharing of the water resources with India hoping its limited capacity to safeguard its interest in the negotiation, which might again go in favour of India. Hence, deliberate efforts were made to block them even at the cost of pushing the development to the back burner. Nepal seemed to be over-cautious on sharing the use of its water resources. To some, Nepal had become so mush anti-India in this respect that it preferred to keep its people in darkness and poverty than letting India utilized the water resources fully for its own benefit. It seems that it had decided to become one-eyed for making India blind.

Problems Ignored:

The government shut its eyes on the fertile lands in Tarai turning gradually into deserts by not taming the rivers as they change their courses frequently causing tension clashes between the peoples living on both sides. The deforestation and unbalanced utilization of Sivalika (Chure) Range Mountains and rivers have brought the beds of rivers up to flood the areas even with meagre rainfall. Nepal appeared detrimental to India getting more water in lean months free of extra cost, irrespective of the fact that the water, which flows abundantly from Nepal in the form of flood, create havoc in India.

5. Matter of Sphere of Influence or Interference in Administration:

The fifth barrier is concerned with the matter of sphere of influence that India is directly or indirectly involved in the Nepalese politics, which is tantamount to Indian interference in Nepal. The restoration of power to the Shah dynasty in the name of democracy by snatching power from the Ranas can be considered to be the first diplomatic endeavour by India to interfere in the internal matters of a country. It was viewed differently by different sectors of Nepal. Some held it as an Indian interference in Nepal. It was led by the Nepalese citizens with support from independent India in the interest of the people of Nepal at large, who were deprived of their all political rights. In other words, to establish democratic rule seemed to be the sole aim of the then Indian government. The then Nepalese establishment was maintaining political cohesion with India by assisting militarily in its hour of needs. But circumstances forced India to take a democratic stand for the greater cause of the people distancing itself from the ruling elite of Kathmandu.

The genesis of Indian interference in Nepal can be traced back to the 1950 Treaty and "Delhi Compromise" which allows India to have a say in several matters pertaing to Nepal. It was believed that ministers were appointed on the advice of Delhi. However, it might have continued only till King Tribhuvan survived. His successor king Mahendra did not toe the Indian line and sought Chinese support to neutralize India in which he succeeded considerably. After his demise, his successor king Birendra tried his best to insulate himself from Indian influence and declared Nepal a zone of peace, which was recognized by more than hundred twenty-five nations except India and the result was obvious. The very motive behind the proposal was to restrict India's influence on facilitating Nepalese leaders to organize their anti-monarchy or democratic movement from the Indian soil. It is generally held the absolute rights of the king were curtailed by the People's movement of 1990, which was indirectly supported by India. It is also believed in some quarters that India was behind the Maoist insurgency, of course, not directly on the logic that the 12-point agreement was reached between the Maoists and the Seven-Part-Alliance in Delhi in November 2005, which paved the way for kickstarting the people's movement-2 to overthrow the monarchy successfully.

Indian Unreal Perception:

Perhaps, India has a policy to invite the new Nepalese head of government whenever there is change of guard in Nepal. Almost all Prime Ministers have visited India in a few months after assuming the office, except a few, like JN Khanal. Actually, these visits have only cosmetic value with no real implications. They simply satisfies India's ego. There may not be any causal relation between political changes in Nepal and Nepalese leaders visiting India.

Question to be Raised:

In this connection, three questions can be raised. - (i) Does India have any political, economic and other leverages over Nepal to force it to follow the latter's advices? (ii) Is Nepal dependent on India for its existence? (iii) Is it psychologically dependent or materially?

It is not difficult to find answers to these questions. Nepal is not really bound by the Treaty of 1950, as its vital provisions have been rendered defunct gradually by Nepal. Its dependence on India for petroleum products and huge gap in the balance of payment in trade and commerce do not force Nepal to toe its line, as Nepal is making payments in foreign currency, which India needs. Nepal seems to be psychologically dependent on India, as it is caused by its past mental impressions.

It was customary to invoke India in different ways in all, big or small and serious or trifle political events. Some have obsession with India as they find India's presence implicitly or explicitly in every vital decision and hold India responsible for getting involved very often in Nepalese politics to some extent. To sum up, this reflects the Nepalese mentality that uses India as an alibi for its ills. Some refer to the appointment of the then CIAA chief Lokman Singh Karki by way of blaming India implicitly and some explicitly. The Nepalese authority directly involved in it knows the real position and it may come out one day in the future.

It seems no wonder that India takes interest in the appointments of Prime Ministers, Home Ministers, and other high officials like Home Secretary and Security Chiefs for it wants a favourable government. Since the border is open, it attaches greatest importance to its security concern. To take interest in the appointments of Minister for Water Resources, appears somewhat tenable to expect favourable decisions. But it was really interesting to know as to why India allegedly took interest in the appointment of the then Chief Commissioner of Commission for the Investigation of Abuse of Authority (CIAA), which had become the bone of contention then.

The previous conception that India engages itself in Nepal's political affairs at the highest level does not hold water, as India's influence has been neutralized gradually by another powerful neighbour China and to a lesser extent by the Western Power Block that are increasingly active in Nepal. Some hold that India has started influencing Nepal at the lower level, as it cannot be effective at the top level.

6. Security:

The sixth barrier is related to security perception. Significantly, the national security dimension acquires prime concern for modern India since its very inception, as it had to deal with Pakistan in its state of Jammu and Kashmir just after its partition. On its realization that high mountains and deep seas cannot safeguard any nation in the twentieth century, it was alert on its northern border too sensing possibility of aggression/ encroachment by the newly born communist China. It did face another challenge in 1962 when there was border conflict with China on the Himalayas and later on with Pakistan in 1965 in full fledged war in its western and eastern sectors. In this connection, S.D.Muni writes," Two sets of perceived security challenges in India have contributed to this development. On the one hand is the deterioration in regional security environment for India, not only as a result of conflicts with China and Pakistan but also due to the expansion of great power military presence in the region.

Internal Problems Posing Security Concern:

On the other hand, India has increasingly experienced internal turmoil and conflict resulting from social unrest and economic imbalances. Some of this turmoil has also tended to acquire secessionist and separatist character involving ethnic and tribal identities. The cases of Assam, Bodo, and Jharkhand movements,

Naga, Mizo and Tripura insurgencies, and Punjab and Gurkha troubles may be mentioned here. The spill-over of similar internal conflicts in the neighbouring countries into India have further complicated India's internal and regional security perceptions." (8)

Muni further states, "Some of the concerns of the Indian State's national security component have directly impinged upon Nepal and India-Nepal relations. India's security concerns towards China and the fallout of internal turmoil in Assam and Darjeeling may be recalled here. The possibility of Sikh terrorists and Bihar and West Bengal based left-extremists (naxalites) seeking shelter in Nepal has occupied attention of India's security managers." (9)

S.D.Muni, who holds the changing global and regional strategic environment as the second important variable since India constitutes the main focus of Super Power policies in South Asia, writes:

"A characteristic feature of Super Power politics in this respect has been that the U.S. and Western policies to cultivate India's neighbours and distance them from India's strategic thrust in relation to regional and global issues. The Soviet Union in order to counter this Western approach, found a convergence with India and thus in endorsing India's perception and approach towards its smaller neighbours. The widening of Sino-Soviet schism and the consolidation of Sino-US rapprochement during the sixties and seventies further strengthened the need for India and the Soviet Union to co-ordinate their regional strategy perceptions. Needless to say that this impact of global great power rivalry got perfectly linked to the regional South Asian conflicts, between India and China and India and Pakistan." (10)

India was skeptic about the role of Nepal in the cold war era. Nepal was having good relations with Pakistan, Sri Lanka. Bangladesh and even with China, which were hostile to it to some extent. Interestingly, in response to the proposal of the Nepalese delegation during king Mahendra's visit to India in August, 1963 for reorganization and modernization of the Nepalese Army, the government of India agreed vide its letter dated January 30, 1965 to give all possible assistance with the object of strengthening the security and independence of Nepal was accepted by the then Royal Nepal Embassy, New Delhi through his letter to Y.D. Gunadevia, Foreign Secretary to the Government of India under the heading of 'Understanding On Import of Arms By Nepal'. (Appendix-3) However, in 1969, the PM Kirtinidhi Bista denounced the Understanding about the import of arms and ammunition and asked India to withdraw Indian technicians and observers(wireless operators) posted on Nepal's northern check posts along the China borders and Military Liaison Officers Group from the Embassy. Finally, India with drew these personnel from Nepal in 1970 as per agreement between the government of India and the Nepalese delegation led by the then Foreign Secretary Yadunath Khanal. Perhaps. Interestingly, king Mahendra declared, in a press interview in October 1970, that Nepal has agreed to:

a. "exchange" military information with India on developments harmful to each other; and -

b. permit the posting of a senior Indian military officer in the embassy in Kathmandu for an "agreed period and job". (11)

Pseudo-Relief:

Perhaps, India succeeded in getting some relief on keeping its officer in the embassy. But this was the greatest setback in the Nepal-India relations. It seemed to happen partly because of the Chinese influence on Nepal and also due to drastic change in the Nepalese perception on Indian concept of its security and also because of Indian establishment's support to anti-royal forces like the Nepali Congress. Unfortunately, the deficit of mutual trust still persists as a stumbling block in getting India's concern over security addressed by Nepal, despite frequent highest-level Nepalese dignitaries' visits to India. And it seems to continue in the days to come too.

Curiously, India perceives that the government of Nepal does not seem to be sensitive towards its security concerns as the Indian fake currency notes continue to come to Nepal from other countries. Terrorists are reported to enter India via Nepal very often. India has been asking for an extradition treaty to control the menace. These issues are of vital concerns for India. It is presumed that since security concerns were not taken up by Nepal seriously, the only alternative before the government of India was to assign responsibility to its security agencies to handle its strategic relation with Nepal.

7. Construction of Roads:

China has been constructing roads in Nepal very strategically since it defined its strategy in Nepal. Coincidently, Nepal decided to link itself with China by road when the Nepali Congress opposed King Mahendra after he dismissed its elected government on 15 December, 1960. It was the period when there was border tension between India and China, which ultimately turned into a bloody conflict in 1962. Against India's warning of communist regime of China, the king's famous reply, "Communism does not travel in cabs" still echoes.

China's first move was to link Kathmandu by Kodari Highway. Unfortunately, it was blocked by the last devastating earthquake in 2015 and the Kerung-Raswa road has been opened, which was used to meet the petroleum supplies during blockade of Indian border. A few days ago, Kor La road has been cleared in the west of the country by the army, which was assigned to carry out the construction work. Kerung is in the middle and Kodari is in the east. And there are half a dozen road construction projects under consideration of the

Chinese Belt and Road Initiative to connect China with India at more than half a dozen points.

Chinese Interests:

There seems to be two reasons for the Chinese interests in roads. First, China may become the first economy of the world superseding United States within a few years. Therefore, it is interested in enlarging its markets for its manufactured goods in very large scale. Nepal cannot be its market destination, as it cannot consume them on large scale because of its limited capacity. It has 28million population. Significantly, about ten million people are out of the country (India and abroad) in search of their bread and butter, and remaining eighteen million people will not be a good market for Chinese goods. Next is India, which is also a fast growing economy in Asia, has more than two-to-three hundred-million population with European standard, can provide a good market for bulk consuming Chinese goods. China may prefer Indian market to the European market. Hence, it may be interested in having many routes through Nepal to reach India.

Secondly, there are border disputes between the two largest populations of the world. India lost the war with China in 1962 and it still claims its huge areas, which are under Chinese occupation. Though these two countries have a mechanism to negotiate and settle the disputes, there is no progress on this score so far. Psychologically, India is always sceptic about China's intention in the region and perceives road constructions by China as a threat to its security, because getting more access to India may be strategically harmful. Interestingly, the plains of Terai/Madhes, which are the adjoining areas of India, have been divided into five fragments in terms of provinces deliberately to link China with India through all these provinces if China so desires.

It is true that China is mightier than India in military strength and economy, but it is equally true that today's India is not the India of 1962. It has also gone from strength to strength all these years and has become one of the biggest economies not only of Asia but also of the world. Nepal, though small in size, has been an Indian market so far. However, it is upto India to see as to how it meets China in Nepal. Significantly, Nepal too will hardly be much benefited by these roads, as these are just the means to transport goods from one place to another, manufacturing country to consuming country. Nepal, which simply falls in between China and India, may not be benefited much as its industries and commerce will not pick up speed in between China and India trade,as has happened earlier through Tibet.

8. Recruitment of Gurkhas in the Indian Army:

The British establishment in India was interested in the recruitment of Gorkhalis in its army, especially after the First World War in which they fought courageously. Their bravery, honesty and their dedication to sacrifice their lives as soldiers, impressed them during their wars that they lodged to capture various parts of Nepal much earlier. It has been mentioned earlier that the bone of contention between the British and the Shah dynasty was the recruitment of Gorkhalis in the British army. Somctimes, they were permitted to recruit when the king or the Regent sought support from them and were denied when there was no favourable king at the helm. Some Rana prime ministers allowed recruitment and some rejected too. In the Second World Wars, Gorkhalis sacrificed their lives but with no satisfactory rewards. Some of them sent back home empty-handed too, which helped the overthrow of the Rana regime, ultimately in 1951.

In August 1947, when India became independent from the British rule, the continuity of Gorkhalis in the Indian army was a problem to be addressed by Both India and the British. Hence, with regard to the recruitment of Gorkhalis, a tripartite agreement (Appendix-4) was reached on the Memorandum dated 7th November 1947 between the Government of Nepal, His Majesty's Government in the United Kingdom, and the Government of the Dominion of India, which was signed at Kathmandu on 9th day of November 1947 by Padma Shamsher Jung B.R. Similarly, A.C.B. Symon for the Government of United Kingdom signed it, and Bedi for the Government of the Dominion of India. The agreement provides for the transfer of all volunteers from Regular battalions of each of the second, sixth, seventh, and tenth Gurkha Rifles leaving the rest with Indian army. There were twenty battalions.

After independence, India too took interest in the continuity, which has been intermittently opposed by the political parties to suit their cause. Even today, the recruitment still continues to remain the bone of contention and the Indian establishment has been taking it as a challenge.

9. Madhes Movement:

The ninth barrier is the so-called Indian support for Madhesi people who have been marginalized for centuries. During the last 250 years and specifically in the last sixty years, barring the last two decades, Nepal does not have any spectacular changes. But after 1951 and especially after 1959, there was gradual industrialization accompanied by urbanization. Kathmandu and other district towns especially situated on the Indian border started developing through smuggling of foreign goods to India by getting huge profit in the trade. Moreover, Indian currency used to flow in Nepal in abundance supporting its economy substantially. With the urbanization, some semi-skilled workers from Tarai and adjoining border areas started coming to Kathmandu for construction jobs requiring a great number of workers, which the local people could not meet. In search of jobs, some vegetable vendors, hawkers and rag pickers came to Kathmandu. They used to send their earned money to their families and hardly any one of them wished to settle here permanently. Of course, before this phase of development took place, some educated persons did come and got settled here. However, some of them took the pioneer job of teaching in schools and colleges in remote hills, plains and the capital.

Historically, Madhesi people are the unfortunate lot, who have been frantically craving for their normal and natural identity in the country, which no other communities like Janajatis and Dalits face. Their nationality is always questioned. The people living on the Nepalese side of the India-Nepal border are being called Madheshis. They have been treated largely as the second grade citizens even when they constitute nearly about forty per cent of the population. On the scale of political power and position, during the last fifty years, Madhesi leaders could not rise above the post of deputy speaker. Of course, in post people's movement 2 of 2006 period, their position has since been elevated to the post of deputy prime minister. They were being given a few seats exceptionally in constitutional bodies and in the diplomatic service. However, their number is getting increased gradually. Ironically, no one was engaged in the erstwhile palace service. Incidentally, the first Constituent Assembly elected Madhesi president and vice president in 2008, due to their strategic election on the basis of number game.

Unfair Treatment to Madhesis:

A few years ago, Madhesis had to go to India for plantation of paddy crops and harvesting the crop depending on India for bread and butter. The practice stopped when young people started going to the gulf countries and Malaysia as migrant workers. Ironically, the fertile land of Tarai is gradually turning into deserts due to deforestation and land erosion taking place by the frequent changes in the courses of rivers, which remained untamed so far. This has been going on for the last four to five decades. The production of food grains has gone down in Madhes. It compels the country to import more food grains from India at increasing prices.

Interestingly, there was a striking change in the attitude of the government since 1970s and onwards. Madhesi students who preferred to go to India for getting education there finding it covenient, were penalized for going there by the government, which used to deduct ten marks from the total marks obtained in the interviews faced by those candidates who applied for government scholarships to have technical education, like B,E and M.B.B.S. etc. Perhaps, this discrimination still continues. Even after 1990s when democracy was restored, the plight of the youths of Madhes has hardly improved. Most of them remain unemployed and do not get jobs in government and semi-government services. The younger generation remains frustrated, as its future appears to be uncertain. Accepting proportional political participation as the only way out to get justified share in political structure and power, they revolted against the establishment through the Madhesi Uprising of 2007 to get Madhes Pradesh to have justified share in the administration. It forced the government to raise the number of seats to be elected for Constituent Assembly proportionally at the cost of more than four dozen innocent lives who were shot dead by the security agencies. It also led to the sharing of seats in the government services.

Protest Begins:

In September 2015, when the new constitution was to be promulgated, its first draft that negated the proportional sharing of seats was published, met with agitations and protests that continued even after the adoption of the constitution by the second Constituent Assembly. Again, more than four dozen of protesters were killed mercilessly by the security agencies leading to 'sit-in' protests at the Nepal-India border, causing blockade of the border.

It was believed that it was directly supported by India for the cause of Madhes. Nepal holds India responsible for the border blockade and called Indian blockade and never accepted it as Madhesi driven, although India used unsuccessfully the border blockades twice in the past for its own purposes. It, thus, takes diplomatic benefit against India in the international community.

Status of Madhesis Questioned:

Ironically, the status of the ordinary Madhesi is sandwiched between Indian and Nepalese perceptions. The issue was overlooked by some foreign scholars and researchers for various reasons. Either they did not have any interests in knowing more about them as it might not come under their scheme of research or deliberately did not go deep into the problem. The situation still continues today. It is evident from the observation of Leo E. Rose, who finds the presence of Madhesi "the large proportion of the Nepali population (20 to25 percent) which is of recent Indian origin," a problem with both ideological and cultural terms for Nepal's national identity. Rose, with regard to Nepal's National Identity problem, writes,

"The Indian republic, on the other hand, poses a different kind of problem in both ideological and cultural terms, particularly in view of India cannot be treated as an alien power in the same way that the British- or the Chinese- can, as Indian influence at all levels, political, economical, cultural and religious, are too persuasive and integral to Nepali society to be ignored or even easily sublimated."(12)

Historical Facts Ignored:

Surprisingly, he does not take trouble in tracing back the history of old settlement of Madhesi community,who were there much before Prithvi Narayan Shah captured those areas from different principalities. There was Simrawn Gadh civilization in Bara district much earlier. It is on records that the rulers of the Makawanpur state, which was captured by Prithvi Narayan Shah before he captured Kathmandu, made land grants to the abbots of different temples. Abbot Ram Das of Janaki Monastry had received land grants from Manik Sen in 1727, Abbot Sital Giri of Kuwan Monastry received grant from Sujagat Sen in 1740, and Abbot Sital Giri received grant from Hem Karan Shah in 1753. (13) There was Sakya dynasty to which Gautam Buddha belonged at Lumbini more than two millennia ago.

Apathy of the British Towards Madhesis:

In contrast to his views, during the British days; the British were almost indifferent towards the original inhabitants, as they did not interfere in their movement from one side to another. They were never particular about their citizenship as they had to recruit Nepalese citizens to their army. India, after independence, considered Madhesis as Nepalese citizen but hardly differentiate between Nepalese and Indian citizens as per 1950 treaty, whereas Nepal never accepted them as real inhabitants or bona fide citizens, considering them as Indians or of Indian origin. It is the stark reality that the government of Nepal issues citizen certificates to them very reluctantly and under compulsion when laws permit them to have it. Madhesis never sought India's cooperation, as it was their birthright.

Madhes and Madhesis not Preferred:

Of course, in recent years, some constructions projects have come up in Terai/Madhes region with Indian aid. Actually, the Indian job is commendable, as these projects, which were over due, could not attract the attention of the Nepalese government. With regard to India's favours to leaders, it appears that it favoured leaders from hill regions more than the leaders from Madhes, except a few who were patronized by the Ministry of External Affairs in the past and may be some in the present. It is quite clear that the sole aim of the Indian diplomacy in Nepal has been to please the leaders of hill origins or the ruling elite in Kathmandu since they always remain at the helm of affairs of the country. Despite Indian appeasement to the ruling elite, India is perceived to favour Madhesis and is apprehended as a danger to undivided Nepal for it may help Madhesis' demand to have a separate country in the long run.

10. Ownership of Buddha:

The tenth barrier, which is more emotional in nature, is the Nepalese citizenship of Buddha. It is an undisputed truth that Buddha was born in Lumbini, which falls under the present political boundary of Nepal. He was born about 2550 years ago. At that time, there was no country like India and definitely Nepal border was not extended to that area. It is a fact that Buddha attained Buddhatva (enlightenment) at Bodha Gaya, now in Bihar state of India. Buddha addressed his disciples describing the Dharma Parivartana Chakra, at Sarnath in Uttar Paradesh, India. Buddha breathed his last at Kushinagar, which too falls in Uttar Pradesh. Before it was confirmed that Lumbini was the birthplace of Buddha, it was being referred to that India was the birth place of Buddha. Though it has been confirmed and accepted world over that Nepal is his birthplace, Nepal still has a bad feeing about India on its previous claim on his birthplace.

11. The Psychology of a Conqueror Mind:

The eleventh barrier is the mindset of the ruler and the ruling class. It was a reality that once Nepal had conquered several principalities in both east and west of present day Nepal. The short history explained earlier (Chapter-2) throws ample light over the issue. The state of Kumayun was captured in 1791 and Gadhwal in 1804-9 and the areas upto Tista in 1777 during Prithvi Narayan Shah. These were taken over by the British in 1815-6, under Sugauli Treaty. (14) The province of Kumaun was under Nepal for 24 years, Garhwal was for a decade and the areas in the east were for nearly four decades (43 years). Nepal, which occupied these areas for very limited periods, still holds that these areas were of Nepal as these were conquered once forgetting the reality that these areas were independent for centuries. The very psychology also plays some role in defining Indian diplomacy in Nepal.

The psychology is a kind of superiority complex from which Nepal suffers. As a matter of fact, a superiority complex is a coping mechanism to deal with an inferiority complex, as someone with a superiority complex asserts one's own feelings of inferiority, which sometimes prove self-delusional. These complexes, which are related to individual human mind, seem effective on social and national psyche too. Nepal feels inferiority complex with India in regard to its vastness of area, population, developmental stage, social engineering, education and scientific achievements, agricultural self-reliance and providing livelihood to thousands of Nepalese citizens.

Superiority Complex of India:

Significantly, India too suffers from superiority complex as it has inferiority complex with regards to other developed and politically powerful countries. Hence its behaviour shows its superiority complex with regard to Nepal. It is to be noted that not every one with an inferiority complex develops a superiority complex, as a superiority complex is only one of many coping mechanisms.

12. Politics of Language:

The twelveth barrier is the supremacy of one language. After capturing Kathmandu valley, the first job of Prithvi Narayan Shah and his successors was to impose Nepali language in administration replacing local Newari Language, which is now called as 'Nepal Bhasha'. Sylvain Levi, accepting the predominance of Hindi in Terai, writes, "In spite of the predominance of Hindi in Terai, the Gorkha language, a mixture of Indian and hilly elements, continued to spread over far off regions of Nepal by dint of the administration and the army". (15)

In Tarai, Hindi was spoken as a common language and still has the same function, as it was difficult for a Madhesi from the east to communicate himself with another Madhesi from the west. In Tarai, Hindi was the medium of teaching. Being the lingua franca, it has unique strength of uniting almost all 20 districts of Tarai/Madhes to form a block. It was the medium through which government officials and educated persons used to communicate with an ordinary person and it still continues because it is difficult for them to communicate themselves either in Maithili or Bhojapuri or in Abadhi. The all pervasiveness of Hindi made not only the ruling elite of Kathmandu including the government and the entire Nepali speaking community scared of Hindi, as may come on the way of unifying Nepal through Nepali language in the form of a monolingual country. They also apprehend, that in the future, Hindi may be a dividing factor of Nepal on the line of language. Thus, through government policy, Hindi was removed as the medium of teaching in schools and colleges. But it failed in separating and dislocating the blood relations existing between the peoples of both sides. The relations have social, cultural, religious, economic, political, strategic, and individual connotations. Hence, the politics of language forms a barrier to have fruitful diplomacy.

References:

1. Rose, L.E., Nepal Strategy for Survival, 1971, pp. 16-17, printed in Nepal, 2010.

2. Mishra, Birendra. P. Nepal-India Relations: Role Played by Psychological Barriers, pub. in The Rising Nepal, 26/11/2011.
3. Kirkpatrick, 'An account of the kingdom of Nepal' pp.147, 153, 280, etc.
4. Slyvian Levy 1905, in his first volume of his book written in French language "Le Nepal" P-31, first volume, Nepali translation).
5. Shaha, Rishikasha, 1992, p-47, Nepal's Foreign Policy: Focus on Nepal-India Relations)
6. Mishra, Birendra P, Group of Eminent Persons, THT, 9/3/2016; THT, Himalyan News Service, THT, 1/3/2019)
7. Muni, S.D. 1992, p-10.
8. Muni, Ibid, pp-10-11
9. Muni, Ibid, p 11.
10. Muni, Ibid, p-46
11. Rose, Ibid P-279-80).
12. Burghart, 2016, p-109, footnote)
13. Regmi Mahesh Chandra, 1999, pp-3-5.
14. Sylvian Levi, Ibid. p-18, First Volume, Nepali translation

4

Chapter

Indian Diplomacy- (1947-64)

Nehru's Personal Diplomacy:

Diplomacy ordinarily means management of a country's foreign policies by its representatives abroad in accordance with the direction of the government (the Ministry of Foreign Affairs). Foreign policy of any country is supposed to be an extension of its domestic policy. However, the domestic policy of a country is at times influenced to some extent by the condition and attitude of its neighbouring countries as well. Peace and prosperity at neighbourhood are more essential in order to have the same in one's country. Significantly, the British colonial Indian diplomacy was virtually getting reshaped by the new real masters of independent India since in 1947. The independent India faced two realities-the growing influence of the western countries on Pakistan, on the one hand, and Tibet, which was brought under the direct control of the Chinese communist regime in 1949, on the other.

Unification of Princely States

Modern India, with its present geographic size, is really the creation of the Independent, India. Before declaring India independent the British declared more than five hundred and sixty princely states as sovereign and empowered them with the right to decide their status in Independent India. It is a fact that the British brought them under its rule after a long military warfare and negotiations with them. Since the British were the immediate masters of India, the new government had the legacy of the British colonial rule. The British Empire had treated Tibet as the buffer state between British India and China. Although China was not so powerful at that time as it is today, yet it was a power to be reckoned with. Previously, British India was not at all scared of independent Nepal for two reasons. First, Nepal, which was an independent kingdom had some specific obligations to act for British India under the Treaty of Sugauli signed in 1815 and also under the Treaty signed in 1923.

In other words, Nepal was an independent kingdom, for the world at large except for British India. Secondly, Tibet was the buffer state between British India and China. The regional balance changed drastically with the emergence of Communist China.

People's Aspiration After World War II:

After the end of the Second World War, there was a wave of getting independence from colonial rules. Nepal could not remain cut off from the air of change blowing in several parts of the globe. India, after becoming independent, supported independence movement in every country including Nepal. The independence movement in India indirectly inspired the enlightened citizens of Nepal to have a democratic setup in place of oligarchic rule of the Ranas. They formed their political outfits during 1947 to 1950 in India as political activities were banned in Nepal by the Rana regime. On the other side, in view of the Indian independence and people's political awareness, jointly made the regime restless to come into action. To meet people's aspiration, the then Rana Prime Minister, Padma Shamsher JBR initiated the political reform by framing a new constitution for the country and held elections to the Rashtra Sabha(National Assembly) in 1949.

Jawaharlal Nehru: As Setter of India's Foreign Policy:

During the early 1950s, democratic India was in its formative stage. It is no exaggeration to state that its first Prime Minister Jawaharlal Nehru was the setter of India's foreign policy, who was the Foreign Minister himself all the time. He was often charged by his opponents of being an idealist, who overlooked the immediate needs of the country and kept engaged himself mostly in international politics for enhancing his own prestige and popularity world over. His approach to Nepal can be divided in two parts. First from1947 to 1960(before the royal takeover of BP Koirala's elected democratic government), and second, after 1961 and onwards.

Personal Idealism and National Realism:

The foreign policy of India seemed to oscillate between the personal idealism and the national realism of Nehru. The personal idealism facilitated the smooth landing of a democratic setup from the oligarchic rule in Nepal when the Rana regime collapsed due to armed revolution led by the Nepali Congress and king Tribhuvan's dissociation from the regime by self-exiling to India. A compromise was reached to have a coalition government of the Ranas and the Nepali Congress headed by its last PM Mohun Shamsher JBR to provide continuity of the government and establish democratic rule by the king by constituting a Constituent Assembly through election to draft a people's constitution after his return from India. All these were the effects of his personal idealism on Indian foreign policy. (1)

Diplomacy Based on Personal Relations:

Against this backdrop, the diplomatic relations between modern India and post-Rana Nepal can be better gauged on the basis of the correspondence between Jawaharlal Nehru, King Tribhuwan and PM MP Koirala during the early 1950s. After the revolt of Raksha Dal, Jawaharlal Nehru, in a personal letter to the king on 27 January, 1952, (2) addressing the king as 'My dear friend', assured that an Indian small party of Army and Air Force officers visiting to Kathmandu; would be of some assistance to Nepal. He writes,

"The whole purpose of this visit is to render assistance, in the shape of advice, where required and not to interfere in any other way with your Government arrangements". To build harmony between the king and the Prime Minister, he writes PM Koirala, enclosing a copy of the letter addressed to the king, on 28 February, 1952. (3) Regarding the internal bickering of the NC and the relation between the two brothers. He writes:

"I spoke quite frankly to him (BP Koirala) about the position in and the needs of Nepal and the great responsibility which rested on a few leading personalities in the movement for freedom in Nepal. These personalities obviously included you and BP. I told him that it was exceedingly injurious to the cause of Nepal, and of course to that of the Nepali Congress, for a conflict to take place between you and him. In fact everybody should have the sense to pull together in this crisis, otherwise they will be swept away."

He Writes Further:

"I told BP that he had some excellent qualities, push, drive, etc., but he was far too impulsive and lacked ballast. No doubt with a little experience he will gain this ballast and be more balanced. He was young and he would have plenty of chances of working for big ends. But by over-reaching himself, he might not only injure his own chances but, what was more important, injure Nepal's interests."

Keeping in view, a presidential contest in the party, he suggests,

"It would be improper for a contested election to take place for the Presidentship of the Nepali Congress. Whoever might win, this would affect the unity of Government and the cooperation of the government with the NC. It would leave a trail of conflict and bitterness behind" He asserts further:

"It was immaterial to me whether the PM was the President of the NC or not. Much could be said for either course. But it was essential that the President of the NC and the PM should pull together... B.P., I think, was impressed by what I said. I said it all in a very friendly way, as I would talk to a young colleague of mine." In the letter dated 23 April 1952, he writes to Koirala,

"It is not for me to advise you in regard to domestic matters but, if I may say so, it might be possible to introduce some simple reforms with great speed. These reforms may relate to the judicial system, which, I understand, is very primitive... May I also say that it would be desirable if the King as well as Ministers did not frequently go out of Nepal, more specially to big cities like Calcutta?"

Nehru's considerate opinion on Nepal was strengthened by his response on the request made by the then Nepalese ambassador to India, General Vijaya Shamsher, the son of Mohun Shamsher, who had resigned from the Prime Ministership. He writes to the new PM MP Koirala on 5 December, 1951 showing respect to Mohun Shamsher as His Highness Maharaja. He suggested the Maharaja not to shift his headquarters to India, but to stay in Nepal and come to India from time to time when he wished. Realizing his difficulties, he writes, "He is an old man now and has seen many changes which naturally have shaken up a great deal. He is entitled to every courtesy and good treatment."

Personal Treatment:

The correspondence between Nehru and PM MP Koirala and king Tribhuvan cited above, surprises one to note that Nehru addresses to the king as a friend and to PM MP Koirala as 'Matrika Prasadji' and also as 'Matrika babu' show his respect and affection to them. From such overtures, one should not hesitate to conclude that Nehru's attitude towards Nepalese dignitaries was that of equals and there was personal touch in his treatment of the Nepalese leaders. Significantly, one can find from the correspondence that serious issues were discussed and Nehru's suggestions were sought not because he was the PM of India but because he was a senior leader known personally to the Nepalese leaders, and he was one of the real well wishers of Nepal among the then Indian establishment and the people.

Nehru Alerts Nepalese Rulers:

The influence of national realism was evident from Nehru's implicit and explicit overtures to the matters relating to Nepal's foreign affairs. He advises Nepalese rulers to be cautious about engaging Americans and Chinese showing his concern over Indian security and also to have a joint approach to foreign policy. Interestingly, despite repeated suggestions cum cautions from Nehru, Nepal succeeded in contacting the Chinese ambassador to India through the then Nepalese Ambassador in August 1954 paving the way for opening diplomatic channel with China.

While cautioning Nepal against employing foreigner and especially regarding US aid, Nehru writes on 25 February, 1952:

"There are all kinds of laws in the US governing help to foreign countries and wanting something in exchange for them. We have been dealing but the US for a long time past and have made it perfectly clear that while help is welcome, we will not have any political or other strings attached to it."

Nehru categorically expresses his commitment not to interfere in the internal matters of Nepal on 6 June, 1952. This he did by writing:

"I have hesitated to write to you because it is none of my business to interfere in any way in the internal politics of Nepal." He attaches importance to two elements in Nepal- stability and promise of progress. He shows his disgust for no progress on holding Constituent Assembly (CA) elections and functioning of the Advisory Council (AC). He writes further:

"These two elements were: the King and the NC... As I know, no progress has been made towards the calling of the CA and the AC has not functioned at all... It is not my concern what kind of Government the Nepalese people would like to have themselves. But if something happens in Nepal, which endangers our own security, then of course this is a matter of great concern to us... History and geography have thrown India and Nepal together. We cannot forget that history or change geography."

Another Caution from Nehru to Nepalese Rulers:

On 31 July 1952, Nehru advises the PM to be broader in outlook:

If I may say so, as PM, you will have to keep this larger viewpoint before you. The country is more important than any individual or group, and it would be a tragedy if, because of group or individual conflicts, the country suffers."

During his second stint as PM, Koirala was advised again by Nehru to be careful about American interference and also become realistic about the takeover of Tibet by China as the whole world has accepted Chinese sovereignty over Tibet (8 May, 1954). He was further advised, perhaps out of the way, not to seek extra-territorial rights and claiming Rs.10, 000 from Tibet and to have mutual consultation with both the countries over foreign affairs. (June 29,1954).

A Summed-up View:

From the above correspondence, one can easily infer some

conclusions regarding India's, especially, of the then PM Nehru 's attitude towards Nepal. First, he wants to see Nepal to grow as an independent democratic country. Secondly, he wants stability in Nepal. Thirdly, he wishes economic development of Nepal. Fourthly, he cautions Nepal against the close relations with China and the United States. Fifthly, he wants Nepal to be serious about the Indian security perception. Sixthly, he does not want any interference in the internal matters of Nepal. And lastly, he has personal goodwill for Nepal and its leaders.

Coup d'etat by King Mahendra in1960

Curiously, Nepal, under the kingship of Mahendra, decided to go against his all good wishes after five years when on 15 December, 1960, King Mahendra dissolved the duly elected Parliament, suspended the constitution and arrested PM BP Koirala and his cabinet colleagues. On the royal coup, Nehru's response was quoted by The Hindu, one of the oldest English daily published in India. It writes on 21 December, 1960," PM Nehru, initiating the debate on foreign affairs in the Rajya Sabha on 20 December, was sharply critical of the Nepal King's dismissal of the Koirala Ministry, suspension of the state's constitution and country-wide arrests and detention of popular leaders. He said the king's sanction came to him not as a surprise but a shock... But the king stated that the king and the Cabinet have not been working harmoniously for some months. He described as "vague" the charges levelled by the king against the Koirala Ministry.

The Koirala Government has been functioning under difficult conditions having regard to the state's history after the elimination of the Rana rule. Of course, nobody could describe the Koirala Government as ideal and for that matter no Government anywhere could be regarded as ideal. The Hindu writes again on 19 January, 1961, thus, "Prime Minister Nehru on 18 January, reiterated his view that the recent development in Nepal was a serious setback to democratic setup. While it was for the people of Nepal to decide what they should do, all that he could say was not 'a step in advance, but a step backward and that step backward will have to be retraced some time or other'. Mr. Nehru was replying to questions at his press conference."

Nehru's Reply to King Mahendra:

Significantly, after a gap of fifty seven years, the letter written by Nehru to King Mahendra (3) throws ample light on India's foreign policy and its diplomacy erasing several doubts and confusions in Nepal. The letter was written by Nehru within two months of the royal takeover on 15 December, 1960, which reiterates his stand on the royal action. It was believed in some quarters in Nepal that the king took over the elected government in consultation with India, as Nehru was not in favour of the continuity of BP Koirala as PM. Presumably, they drew their conclusion on the premise that there were no serious responses by way of any action from India against the royal move.

Nehru's True Conviction:

Interestingly, Nehru does not initiate any correspondence with the king as he realizes that what have happened in Nepal are in opposition to his wishes and trust. He writes only in response to the letter written to him by king Mahendra. The very acknowledgement of the letter speaks more about the fact. He writes that the king has tried to inform him about the royal action taken at his pleasure hardly needs his response. Moreover, he replies his letter after meeting Minister Dr. Tulsi Giri through whom he could learn about the situation prevailing in Nepal. He writes that they had a long discussion for about two hours. Minister Giri informed him about the king's views regarding the present condition and he too shared his personal views with Giri. He takes it as a freedom to write the king about the subject they talked, although he believes that Giri might have informed the king about the subject - matters of their discussion. He writes that he is writing to him with full confidence in each other.

Explicit Foreign Policy:

He begins his letter narrating briefly his own past performances that made him prime minster of India with socialist outlook having strong antagonism to the thinking of accumulating excess wealth through personal effort in trade, commerce and industry, virtually becoming an anti-feudalist. He writes that only history will judge his success and failure accepting the fact he has failed in many respects. He writes about the Indian policy towards Nepal very candidly, which was already communicated to king Tribhuvan and prime minster MP Koirala long back. He writes frankly that in early days of independence, the question of what to do about Nepal came up and they decided for an independent Nepal knowingly that its independence was virtually curtailed by the British for all practical purposes with regard to its foreign relations. British ambassadors used to play important roles. His respected father (king Tribhuvan) and the then Rana prime minster told him that a British Ambassador had to flee to India on account of some of his activities.

Thinking of Indian Leaders:

They (Indian leaders) wished Nepal an inseparably independent and self-reliant country, which was natural and pragmatic as well. So, they at once accepted full independence. Their only concern in Nepal was its independence, which was also evident from their present policy. Simultaneously, they felt that their (Nepal and India) past history, culture and geography have made them inseparably closed to each other and in some subjects, primarily in foreign affairs and defence, and Nepal and India could build deep relations through negotiations, which was in the interest of both countries.

Nehru's Reference to The Past:

He, recalling the past, adds that they had their first old treaty with the Ranas. Knowing well that they (Indian leaders) disagreed with the then government regarding the outlines of political and economic policies, they did not think proper to interfere. Later, they learnt that his father was liberal that made them happy. He narrates further about his father's visit to Delhi, who was welcomed as a honourable guest. To negotiate the internal problem on the request from the Ranas, with their (Indian) felicitation, since they (Indian leaders) were eager to see a stable and progressive government in Nepal, a compromise was reached and the king returned home and a coalition government was formed. To start with, the continuity of government was accepted as the Rana prime minster continued. Sadly, Prime Minster's continuity could not be possible further and thereafter there was continued change of guard with public assurance to provide a democratic setup, hold periodic elections and adopt some from of parliamentary governments. Nepal faced many challenges including shortages of trained government servants. Whenever they were requested, they tried their best to help without any intention of any kind of intervention.

Importance of King and Nepali Congress Reminded:

After the king ascended to the throne, they became glad to learn about king's decision to frame a new constitution, hold election and form a democratic government. They believed that it was the only proper wayout. The king kept his words to the people, conducted election and formed government as per mandate. It was a matter of two years back, in view the problems faced then, the voting was fruitful and with its results, a strong party with massive majority emerged.

Addressing him as His Majesty, Nehru reminds the king that he told His Majesty so many times that there were only two stable factors in Nepal. First, King and second, the Nepali Congress, which was the only established political party with popular support. For Nepal, being the least developed country, it was not possible for any one of the two to succeed on its own strength against odds. For this reason, he felt it essential that these two factors should cooperate with each other; otherwise there would be continuity of regression and instability. He stresses on it that any tussle between the two would be harmful to Nepal. At least twice, the king told him that the king was not satisfied with the method of functioning of the government due to blooming corruption and unsatisfactory working of the administration. It was painful to him to listen it. But he remembers that for these failures, previous administration and the backwardness of the country by all means were also responsible. To solve the problem, the only wayout was to develop the country and fight with corruption and maladministration.

Actually, no great change is possible without people's vast support and cooperation. Even from far away, he understands that the last government amidst all failures has also brought great reforms in the old administration sector and apart from these, it has opened the doors of additional reform and progress.

Nehru's Anguish:

With regard to the royal takeover on December 15, 1960; he writes that he is greatly distressed by king's proclamation of the dissolution of the government and both Houses of parliamentant and taking over the reigns of the country. On account of his life-long training, thinking and his indispensable inner conviction, he says that these steps cannot lead the king to king's goal, which he has communicated to the people. Neither his government nor he has any intention to interfere in Nepal. He answered all queries on Nepal in a controlled and disciplined manner as per parliamentary practices. Apart from his displeasure on series of events taking place, he was anxious about the unfair and wrong propaganda in the Nepalese media. Some of the allegations were unjust and disrespectful. The allegations were amusing and encouraging. All these showed that these were happening either with the instructions of the government or its silence.

Democracy and Development:

With regard to the present conditions and king's thinking for the future, Dr. Giri told him that king's goal was to achieve democracy for which king wanted to have economic development as its first condition. To him, he writes:

Development Without Democracy Not Possible:

Economic development is a long-time process and a troublesome issue. It has to be developed through well-established civil movement, efficient governance, cooperation with the administration, and special planning with fixed goal. Pointing out the Nepalese constraints of development like a dearth of trained human resources and continuity of old method of administration, apart from lagging behind in education, he doubts the pace of development. Neither the world nor any country will remain static. If any country does not go ahead with speed, it will engulf in social and political crises, which will be the carrior of repeated crisis and obstruct the progress. For this reason, he fails to understand that when Nepal will in continued crisis, how will it have remarkable economic development? The country will be trapped in deadlock and the energy of the country will be spent on conflict, which will make the country weak. So, he does not visualize the progressive setup and stability of the government, if present condition continues. He anticipates that the situation may worsen further and the king and his country have to face greater problems. In such a time of crisis, the king may think of external help and he may get it, but it will create new risk and weakness for the country.

Nehru Cautions Nepal Against China:

While referring to its two neighbours-India and China, he asserts that Nepal is related to India in respects of religion, culture, history and geography. These are the permanent features which cannot be changed with the flow of time. So far as India is concerned, they (Indian leaders) are trained in such a way that they cannot attack and be aggressive on the border. Their whole structure and the structure of government and people will oppose it. We cannot get anything from it. On the contrary, China has a different system and working style. Presently, its working method is aggressive. Tough they always want friendly relations with this great country; it has adopted its aggressive policy, which they cannot tolerate. They, however, have adopted the goal of maintaining friendly relations with China.

Nehru cautions Nepal by telling that the condition of Nepal is different. It is weak and may be incapable of meeting any risk from its northern border. China may try to have friendly relations with the king to keep Nepal distant from India. It is upto the king to think whether its relations with China with whom it has least common interests, would be in the interest of Nepal or not. Indian leaders feel that Nepal's friendly relations with India, may deter any aggression from China. He is, therefore, serious about the present activities and feels if such activities continues, these may invite internal conflict. To return to the democratic setup at the earliest is the only wayout from this entanglement. The more it is delayed, Nepal has to face unfavourable situations. There would be no constitutional progress till this path remains closed. Thereafter people may demonstrate unconstitutionally and Nepal will be entrapped in the whirlwind of civil war.

King Advised About the Future:

He writes further that he is trying to write the king quite earnestly because of their great friendship and confidence. This friendship is essential also in the interest of both Nepal and India. As he has said earlier, they (Indian leaders) have neither any intention nor any wish to interfere. Their main interest is in the development of an independent and democratic Nepal. Naturally, they are also interested in their defence as the activities in Nepal may also affect them. For this reason, he seriously requests His Majesty to think of not only by perceiving the present condition but also in view of the future, which will open up itself. He may dare to advise the king that the present crisis should not be allowed to continue and steps should be taken to empower citizens to express their views. If the present parliament cannot be recalled, fresh elections can be held. If there is corruption, it can be acted upon harshly. If the administration is bad, it can be made right, but there is no chance of satisfying the people by ambiguous and doubtful allegations. He draws the attention of the king towards foreign media including the British and writes that Britain is quite favourable to the king, but he might have read the criticisms published in the media there. Today's world opinion cannot tolerate easily the regression of the democratic process.

Nehru's Endeavour to Improve Relations:

After the royal coup, hundreds of leaders and workers of the banned Nepali Congress took shelter in India and started their armed protests against the government. India, being a democratic country could not control them strictly as the borders between Nepal and India were open. The official relations got soured. Mean time, the tension on the India-China borders, which was brewing for quite some time, ultimately resulted in a war between China and India in 1962. Nehru sent a team under the leadership of Lal Bahadur Shashtri that consisted of Dr. Karan Singh, and Bhagwan Sahay to Kathmandu on unofficial visit in 1963 to redefine the relationship between Nepal and India. Shastri played a crucial role in putting some restrictions on the Nepali Congress and its workers, who had waged armed movement from India against the government as its leaders including the duly elected PM BP Koirala were behind bars. The NC ultimately stopped its activities. And the NC armed cadres were asked to maintain the distance of 20 KM from the international border.

India and Constituent Assembly (CA):

The issue of the Constituent Assembly was brought by India to base the democratic setup in Nepal. Since India's diplomacy was democracy-centric, it was for a democratic Nepal from the very beginning of the epochal political change in Nepal in early 1950s. King Tribhuvan, while self-exiled in India (took refuge in the Indian Embassy on 9 November, was flown to Delhi on 10 November, 1950) accepted an Indian memorandum proposing a compromise formula after negotiating with the two ministers of the Rana Government, Bijaya Shamsher and Keshar Shamsher, the foreign and defence ministers respectively who returned to Kathmandu for finalizing the following three-point formula on 8 December, 1950:

Three point formula of diplomatic relations:

(i) An elected Constituent Assembly(CA) to draft a new constitution;

(ii) An interim government with "popular" (with Nepali Congress) representation but a Rana prime minister; and

(iii) Recognition of King Tribhuvan.

After a long deliberation, an agreement was signed on 7 February, 1951 in Delhi. (4)

CA Adopts Constitution After 64 Years:

Finally, after a lapse of sixty-four years, Nepal succeeded in getting its constitution duly adopted by the second CA on 20 September, 2015, as the first elected CA was dissolved without adopting a constitution. Historically, the first call to have an elected CA was made by the late king Tribhuvan, as stated above. After all, it is asked as to who initiated the agenda of CA in the "Delhi Compromise?" There were four main political stakeholders in Nepal at that time. The first stakeholder was the king, second was the Rana Prime Minster, the third was the Nepali Congress (NC) which had waged an armed struggle against the Rana regime and the last was the facilitator, the Indian establishment. The king could not be the originator of the idea of an elected CA, as he might not have an idea about any CA, since he was almost captive in his own palace from his very childhood. Moreover, had it been his project, he could have done some thing at least to hold CA election before his death in Switzerland in February 1955. After his demise his successors too did not take interest in it as they might have apprehended of losing their absolute power. The Ranas too could not have proposed a CA as they had already got a constitution drafted by some Indian experts a few years ago, which did not have any mention of it. Similarly, the NC too could not be regarded as its proposer, as BP Koirala, in his 'Atmavritanta'(autobiography) himself admits that -

No NC leaders including Koirala Brothers (MP Koirala and himself) were allowed to have direct negotiation with the exiled king at the Hyderabad House in new Delhi to discuss about the contents of the 'Delhi Compromise'. He simply calls it, "an imaginary matter."(5) Ultimately, it was Nehru who would have intended to see Nepal to be governed democratically on the basis of a new constitution drafted by an elected CA.

Agenda of CA Ignored:

Sadly, the agenda of the CA was not entertained even by the people's movement of 1990, which failed in meeting the ambitions of the people as it accepted constitutional monarchy through the new constitution drafted by the representatives of the NC, CPN –UML and the nominees of the then king in 1990. However, Gajendra Narayan Singh of Sadbhavana Party raised the issue of CA for having a people's constitution sharing the state power of the kingdom by all communities including the marginized Madhesis. Sadly, he too did not stick to his demand due to his limited political sphere and his lack of political shrewdness to fight for this just cause.

Maoists Commitment For CA:

The Maoists, who raised arms against the state in early 1996, took up the issue of CA while negotiating peace with the government. Finally, they had come out with three main demands:

Maoists Demands:

a. to hold round table national conference,
b. to form of a strong coalition government and
c. to hold the CA election.

Maoist Agenda for CA Examined:

It was, however, a matter of curiosity as to why did the Maoists demand CA being adherent to the political thought of one party rule and the dictatorship of the proletariat. Were the Maoist leaders under the influence of Indian leaders, both the leftist and the democratic, during their stay in India earlier and during insurgency? Or did they think of copying Indian democratic innovations for themselves? It is surprising as to how the communists, who had their schooling in Marxism, believing that power comes out of barrel of the gun, could advocate for CA election where the secret ballots count and not the bullets. Perhaps, before the Maoist leaders had their schooling in Marxism, their original mindset remained by and large democratic, which influenced their political thinking of democratic innovation even after joining the Marxist path. Alternatively, some of the Maoist leaders, who were basically democrat, initiated and convinced their colleagues to go for an elected CA, a more democratic process to carry the people's wish ultimately.

References:

1. Mishra, Birendra Prasad, art. Bend in the river, pub. in Republica, 6/10/2012.
2. Appendixed to the book 'MP Koirala, A role in a revolution', published in 2008, pp. 203-4.
3. Ibid, P-208-10
4. Its Nepali translation by Pradeep Giri, a Nepali Congress MP has been published in the Nepali daily, ' Naya Patrika' on 3 November 2018.
5. Rose, Ibid, p-193.
6. Koirala B.P. Atmavritant, 2055 BS, p. 146).

5

Chapter

Post-Nehru Diplomacy

The post-Nehru period of diplomacy has covered the names of those Prime Ministers who have contributed, even least, to the Indian diplomacy in Nepal. However, following were the prime ministers:

1. Lal Bahadur Shastri, 1964-66.
2. Indira Gandhi, 1966-77,
3. Morarji Desai, 1977-79.
4. Charan Singh, 1979-1980.
5. Indira Gandhi, 1980-84.
6. Rajiv Gandhi, 1984-1989.
7. Vishwanath Pratap Singh, 1989-1990.
8. Chandra Shekhar, 1990-1991.
9. P V.Narasimha Rao, 1991-96.
10. Atal Bihari Vajpayee, 1996-1996.
11. H. D. Deve Gowda, 1996-1997.
12. I.K. Gujral, 1997-1998.
12. Atal Bihari Vajpayee, 1998-2004.

Lal Bahadur Shastri's Reconciliatory Diplomacy:

After the demise of Pt. Nehru on 27 May, 1964, he became the PM of India. Sadly, he was the PM hardly for 18 months, as he died at

Tashkant in early January 1966 where he had gone to negotiate with Pakistan under the mediation of Russia. During his short period of prime ministership, he was preoccupied mostly with the tensed relations with Pakistan that ultimately resulted in war with Pakistan in1965 in which India captured substantial portion of land in Pakistan. The post-war period too kept him engaged in negotiations with Pakistan. Inspite of his engagement with Pakistan, he spared time to improve relations with Nepal, which was not so smooth. He secretly concluded the Treaty of Arms Assistance Agreement on 30 January 1965 with Nepal regarding supply of arms and ammunition to the Nepalese army. Interestingly, Nehru had full confidence in him and as a troubleshooter Nehru involved him in negotiation with Nepal and Sri Lanka on crucial issues. In response to the Indian support to the Nepali Congress workers taking up arms against the government from India and apprehending Indian domination and influence of Tarai, King Mahendra got started the construction of Kodari Raj Marg (High Way) linking China through the autonomous region of Tibet with Chinese support. The construction of the East-West Highway (Mahendra Raj Marg) in Tarai region was also initiated.

In this context, he was also deputed by Nehru in 1963 to negotiate with Nepal to see how India's interests of security could be safeguarded. And perhaps, the negotiation, which he had started, culminated in signing of the treaty in 1965 during his regime. PM Shastri sent Srimman Narayan as an ambassador to Nepal. Narayan with his courteous behaviour, succeeded in getting king's balanced treatment against Nepal's growing dependence on China through the treaty of 1965.

Indira Gandhi's Aggressive Diplomacy:

After the sudden demise of prime minister LB Shastri, Indira Gandhi, who was the Information and Broadcasting Minister in

Shastri's Cabinet' was elected PM after defeating a senior most leader, Morarji Desai in Congress Parliamentary party election for leadership. She was PM for nearly 12 years. During that period, the relations that got strained during the last days of Nehru continued to remain the same by and large.

She visited Nepal in 1966 to improve India's strained relations with Nepal, but proved to be of no avail. In 1969, when PM Kritinidhi Bista denounced, in unequivocal terms, the Arms Assistance Agreement and called the Treaty of 1950 had fallen into disuse as India did not consult Nepal in 1962 and 1965 wars was no longer biding on either party and also demanded for withdrawal of Indian wireless operators from Nepal-China border and the Indian Military Liaison Group, the Indian Foreign Minister Dinesh Singh threatened to close the borders formally. To improve the strained bilateral relations the Nepalese delegation led by Foreign Secretary, Yadu Nath Khanal visited Delhi in September 1969. Secretary Khanal succeeded in getting the joint statement issued that emphasized the existence of 'an identity of interests and 'of mutual understanding, trust and confidence' between the government, and the people of Nepal and India. It was on the basis of this understanding the Indian Military Liaison Group and the Indian wireless operators were withdrawn by August 1970. (1) It had direct impact on the extension process of the 'Trade and transit treaty of 1960 as it was not concluded on due date, though no supplies were affected. After the return of Indira Gandhi with a thumping majority in parliament in 1971 election, Nepal had to sign the treaty on less favourable terms.

After signing of 25-year Peace and Friendship treaty with Russia, India helped East Pakistan to declare itself independent Bangladesh in 1971 by bifurcating it from Pakistan, Nepal was the second country to recognize Bangladesh after Bhutan did it. It is believed that the recognition by Nepal took toll upon the health of king Mahendra fatally. King Birendra succeeded king Mahendra after his demise. Significantly, Indira Gandhi had appointed a political figure Raj Bahadur as an ambassador to deal with Nepal politically.

Interestingly, king Birendra launched his proposal for declaring Nepal - a zone of peace at his coronation in 1974. The king introduced a proposal to declare Nepal as a zone of peace to neutralize the provisions of the Treaty of Friendship of 1950. More than hundred countries recognized the proposal but on doing so, nothing tangible was achieved by Nepal. Since India did not recognize the proposal, it ultimately fell flat after the people's movement of 1990.

Indira Gandhi Faced Hostility:

She had to face a hostility on two fronts, first a hostile government and second a political leader ex-premier BP Koirala, a friend and supporter of Jaya Praksh Narayan who had spear-headed the movement against Indira Gandhi whose election was declared invalid by a high Court. She was not willing to relinquish her post and declared the state of emergency in the country to continue as Prime Minister. She could not deal with Koirala and the King simultaneously that jeopardized her diplomacy towards Nepal. King was not kind to her because she had given shelter to Koirala and Koirala was not favourable to her because he was against the political leadership of Indira Gandhi and perhaps, also of Nehru who could not save his elected government and his arrest in 1960.

Morarji Desai's Easy Diplomacy:

He became Prime Minister in 1977 when Indira Gandhi and the Congress party got defeated in 1977's general election that was conducted after six years, as the tenure of the Lower House was extended by one year during the Emergency proclaimed by her in 1975. There was a wave against Indira Gandhi and she lost the election miserably. The then Janta Party government was formed under the leadership of Desai. Sadly, his government could hardly last for two and half years, as it collapsed due to his party's internal bickering. However, during the short span of regime, he visited Nepal and declared from a public platform that he was ready to sign as many agreements with Nepal as it wanted. And ultimately, by playing an easy diplomacy, two separate agreements for Trade and Transit, were signed fulfilling the demand of Nepal.

Second Inning of Indira Gandhi:

The Morarji Desai government collapsed due to internal conflict of the Janta party. There was dissension in the party opposing the authority of Desai reducing his majority in the House. A faction led by Charan Singh, who formed a party named Lok Dal, claimed majority with support from the Congress Party. Charan Singh took the oath as Prime Minster in 1979. But his government could not seek the confidence of the House as Congress Party withdrew its support. However, Singh resigned and recommended the dissolution of Lok Sabha and called for another general election in January 1980 to have a new government with fresh mandate of the people.

In the 1980 general election, the Congress party under Indira Gandhi came out victorious and assumed power again in 1980. The result of the election was against the unstable government and the internal bickering of the Janta Party that had come to power against the state of emergency declared by Indira Gandhi in 1975.

Engaged in Domestic Problems:

During her second stint as Prime Minster, she was busy with domestic problem like Khalistan movement and liberation of the golden temple from Bhindranwale killing him in the temple under

Operation Blue Star that led to her assassination by her Sikh security guards before completing her term. This paved the way for her son Rajiv Gandhi to succeed her. Significantly, to deal with Nepal, she deputed an experienced bureaucrat H.C.Sarin as ambassador who was governor of Andhra Pradesh and a state in the North East.

Rajiv Gandhi's Performing Diplomacy:

Immediately after assuming office, he called for another general election in which his party won with more than two-thirds majority. He took some daring internal and external decisions like sending humanitarian relief packages to Tamil rebellions in the war-torn regions of Sri Lanka by air and deploying naval ships to Maldives to free it from robbers who had captured some islands. Similarly, He visited Nepal to attend the SAARC summit and gave it a reality. The issue of two separate agreements for trade and transit surfaced again during his Prime Ministership, as the term of trade agreement, which had expired, needed extension. In the absence of trade agreement, there was stoppage of supplies from India, a kind of economic blockade, which continued for several months. People suffered a lot on account of the economic blockade. However, the shortages of essential goods created resentment among the common people that hastened the People's Movement of 1990 that threw away the partyless Panchayat regime after almost three decades.

Vishwanath Pratap Singh:

VP Singh succeeded Rajiv Gandhi in 1989 when the Congress party led by Gandhi got defeated in the general election on the charges of corruption. VP Singh, who was the Finance Minister in Rajiv Gandhi's cabinet, resigned and spearheaded a campaign against Rajiv Gandhi charging him of taking bribe in purchase of Bofors guns. His party had no clear-cut majority in the Lower House. He, however, formed the government supported by the B.J,P, from outside. His government lasted from 2 December, 1989 to 10 November, 1990. Coincidentally, there was people's movement in Nepal in 1990, which threw away the partyless Panchayet system. An Interim government was formed under the leadership of K P Bhattarai. During the visit of Bharrarai to Delhi; the issue of trade and transit was solved as India agreed to sign two separate treaties. Nepal too agreed to certain Indian concerns like equal treatment to Indian teachers working in Nepal and on custom duty imposed on Indian goods. Interestingly, I K Gujral was the Foreign Minister in his cabinet pursuing his own foreign policy.

P. V. Narasimha Rao's Quiet Diplomacy:

Chandra Shekhar succeeded V.P. Singh as Prime Minister. His government was supported by the Congress Party, which withdrew its support on the charges of spying on its leaders by his government. His government lasted from November10, 1990 to June 21, 1991. He resigned and dissolved Lok Sabha for people's fresh mandate.

Narsimha Rao succeeded Chandra Shekhar as prime minister. In the general election, which was held after Chanra Shekhar dissolved the Lower House, the Congress party won significant seats in the House. PV Narshimha Rao with support from some fringe parties, became Prime Minister who governed India for five years. It is believed that the main reason for winning considerable seats was the sympathy votes for the Congress as its president and former Prime Minister Rajiv Gandhi was assassinated by the LTTE of Sri Lanka before the second phase of the polling.

Narasimha Rao Smoothened Relations:

He visited Nepal and signed an agreement on the Mahakali Integrated Project and the Pancheshwar multi-purpose project with Nepal, when there was minority government in Nepal led by CPN-UML leader Manmohan Adhikari. The India-Nepal relations were some what soured with the issue of Mahakali Project completed by India unilaterally. Although PM G.P Koirala 's government, which was formed in 1991 after the first people's movement of 1990, had signed a Memorandum of Understanding on Mahakali river, which became controversial in Nepalese political circle. The Supreme Court of Nepal asked the government to get it approved by two-thirds majority. It was approved by the Nepalese parliament later.

I.K. Gujral's Liberal Diplomacy:

H.D.Deve Gowda succeeded Atal Bihari Vajpayee, who could not cobble together fringe parties to have a majority to continue his government. His government lost the vote of confidence. He was in the office from 1 June, 1996 to April, 1997.

I.K. Gujral was the third Prime Minister of the 11th Lok Sabha succeeding Deve Gowda. He had the support of the Congress Party. He remained in the office form 21 April, 1997 to 19 March, 1998. His tenure was short as the Congress party withdrew its support. Inspite of his limited time of performance, he crafted his own foreign policy especially the neighbourhood policy, which was termed as 'Gujral Doctrine'. He was also a two-time foreign Minister. It seems that he developed his policy during his foreign ministership while dealing with the neighbouring countries. It was always questioned whether the doctrine was really a doctrine at all or simply an idea, which he harboured and tried to implement during his short regime.

On 20 January, 1997, while speaking on "Aspects of India's Foreign Policy", at the Bandaranaike Centre for International Studies, Colombo, he himself tried to define his doctrine, "The 'Gujaral Doctrine' if I may call it so, states that, first, with its neighbours like Bangladesh, Bhutan, Maldives, Nepal and Sri Lanka, India does not ask for reciprocity, but gives and accommodates what it can in good faith and trust. Second, we believe that no South Asian country should allow its territory to be used against the interests of another country of the region. Third, that none should interfere in the internal affairs of another. Fourth, all South Asian countries must respect each other's territorial integrity and sovereignty. And finally, they should settle all their disputes through peaceful bilateral negotiations." (2)

Five Points Evaluated:

Out of all these five points, the first was unique and the rest were the common basic tenets of international relations to govern the foreign policy of any nation. It is easy to have a general foreign policy relating to far off nations, but to chart out a foreign policy determining relations with neighbours, is really a tedious task. To have good relations with the neighbours is the prime duty of any government, whether it is a hostile nation or a friendly. No nation has any option to choose its neighbours. It is, in this context, said that geography cannot be altered and history cannot be forgotten. Gujral, during his brief tenure, was most probably governed by his sentiments to carve a place second to Nehru for himself in giving a different direction to the foreign policy of India in and through propagating and setting an ideal tone in its neighbourhood. Perhaps, he forgot the reality of geographic situations and political conditions that influenced the relations between the two nations significantly.

Atal Bihari Vajpayee's Developmental Diplomacy:

A.B. Vajpayee has a unique identity of becoming Prime Minster of India thrice during his total six years in the office. In 1996, he became Prime Minster for the first time and remained in the office from 16 May, 1996 to June 1996. He resigned, as he could not show majority in the House. It was the shortest government. He became Prime Minister second time in 1998, but he was forced to dissolve the Lower House (Lok Sabha) in 1999 due to the withdrawal of support by its major alley the AIDMK calling for another general election in which his party, the B.J.P. came out victorious with a substantial number of seats. He, again, formed a coalition government of several fringe parties under 'National Democratic Alliance' and took the oath of Prime Minister for the third time. His government lasted till 22 May, 2004.

Vajpayee Faced Difficult Situation:

During his tenure, he visited Nepal to attend the SAARC submit in 2002. During his tenure, the Nepal-India relations appeared smooth Some extra ordinary events in Nepal did not allow his diplomacy to be effective. The Maoist insurgency did not allow the relations to improve, as it was generally held that the Maoists were backed by India. Further, King Birendra and his family were assassinated in 2001 and the ex-king Gyanendra assumed the state power to rule the country directly. He put senior political leaders behind bars. All these restricted the scope of Indian diplomacy. Significantly, it is during PM Vajapayee tenure, the Nepalese Maoists committed to support to India through the letter written to the Indian PMO in 2003.

Interestingly, there was a kind shift in India's attitude towards the development of Terai, as construction project of schools were taken up by India in accordance with the agreement during S. B. Deuba's visit to India authorizing the Indian embassy to complete project upto 30 million directly in consultation with the District Development Office of Nepal under revolving fund provided by India. This was really a blessing in disguise as dozens of schools, which were in dire need of buildings to provide education to the youth. Gradually, such projects were also taken up in hill and high mountain regions. The scheme is still continuing.

References:

1. Shaha, Rishikesha, pp-38-39
2. Mishra, Birendra, Prasad, art. The Gujral Doctrine, pub. in The Himalyan Times, on 30/1/2013.

❖ ❖ ❖

6

Chapter

Dr. Manmohan Singh's Indirect Diplomacy (2004-14)

Dr. Manmohan Singh, who was chosen as the Prime Minster of India in 2004 by the then Congress president Sonia Gandhi when her party emerged as the single largest party in the House of Representatives (Lok Sabha), led the government for ten years. He was the finance Minister in the PV Narshimha Rao government and steered the economy by his liberal policy with his experience as the Deputy Chairman of the Planning Commission, and also as the Governor of the Reserve Bank of India.

Situation In Nepal:

At the time of Dr. Singh assuming office of Prime Minister in 2004, Nepal was going through the Maoist insurgency, which was the matter of prime concern for India. The Maoists and the State were fighting to finish each other by continuously engaged in inflicting severe military losses to each other by augmenting arm supplies from different sources. However, the supplies of arms and ammunitions to the army were on hold by India, the US and the UK since 1 February, 2005 when the king took over the reigns of the kingdom by forming cabinet under his own chairmanship. Only during the first week of July, 2005; the first shipment of non- lethal arm supply consisting of 20 military jeeps, bulletproof jackets, and Mine-

Protected Vehicles etc., had reached from India and the US army had resumed training to army personnel. (1) The clashes between the army and the Maoists continued unabated forcing innocent people to bear the brunt of the civil war for the last nine years.

It was commonly held that the prolonged insurgency in Nepal had become a thorny issue for India too. The then Maoist activities in Sitamarhi, Sheohar and East Champaran and other districts of Bihar definitely were alarming. It was believed that about one hundred and seventy five districts of the nine states of India were affected by the Indian Naxals and PWGs, who were having links with the Nepalese Maoists. Hence it seemed imperative for the government of India to take suitable measures for curbing activities of the Nepalese Maoists in adjoining border areas and other places. However, it was interesting that Nepalese leaders used to meet the Maoist leaders at several places such as Silliguri, Lucknow, and Delhi and even Dr. Baburam Bhattarai, an one-time supremo of the party, used to stay and discuss with Indian and Nepalese leaders in Delhi. To some, because of open border, the Maoists took advantages of not only taking shelter in India when pressure was mounted on them by the security personnel but also took replenishment of arms and ammunitions from there.

Security Main Concern of Diplomacy:

In short, it seemed that the diplomatic relations were gradually replaced by the concern of India about its security as it was hardly assured of by Nepal. There was a deviation in Indian approach of dealing with the then establishment, as the Indian diplomacy suffered further set back when the king sought Chinese membership of SAARC at Dhaka Summit. These two factors might have prompted India to deal with the Maoists cautiously taking so much time in getting the Maoist above board by making it a signatory to the 12-Point Understanding with the Seven- Party Alliance of

Nepal in November 2005 in India. Curiously, the Nepalese parties claimed to have negotiated with the Maoists themselves without any assistance from India.

Political Fluidity in Nepal:

PM Singh often charged with the allegation that he did not visit Nepal, despite different Nepalese Prime Ministers visited India from time to time. During his period, there were changes of guard about a dozen times. There were transitions from the elected government to the direct rule of the king and from restoration of democracy to the election to the Constituent Assembly and from monarchy to republic. Also, perhaps, owing to his bureaucratic temperament, he followed indirect diplomacy. Foreign Ministers were made to visit Nepal often. Natwar Singh was sent to Nepal within weeks of his assuming the charge of the ministry in 2004. Before the CPM withdrew support to the United Progressive Alliance government in 2008, Communist Party of India-Marxist leader, Sitaram Yachury happened to be the link between the Nepalese political parties and the Ministry of External Affairs. There after, a group of three Congress MPs, under the leadership of the Congress general secretary Digvijya Singh, had visited Nepal to acquaint themselves with the political situation in Nepal. Later, Pranab Mukherjee, after appointed as the Foreign Minister, visited Nepal in November 2008.

Second Innings of PM Singh:

During the second innings of Dr. Manmohan Singh as Prime Minister of India, the Indian External Affairs Minister SM Krishna paid his first visit to Nepal from 15 to 17 January, 2010. (2) He had meetings with all high ranking dignitaries, discussing political issues with his Nepalese counterpart, signed five Memoranda of Understanding and got released a joint communiqué accepting terrorism and extremism as a common threat for both the countries apart from dwelling on ways to enhance security measures to control smuggling of fake Indian currency notes, cross border crimes etc.

Change of Guard:

Significantly, there was a coalition government led by PM Madhav Kumar Nepal of CPN-UML with the Nepali Congress as the main coalition partner, the Madhesi ganaadhikar Forum(democratic), the Tarai Madhes Lokatrantic Party and others were as coalition partners. He also met the president of the UCPN-Maoist, PK Dahal. 'Prachanda' who got a chance to put-forward his demands before him, as he claimed to have direct talk with New Delhi. However, its impacts are yet to be known as he demanded cancellation of treaties like 1950 treaty on the one hand and indirectly sought India's favour too for his reinstatement as PM on the basis of the people' mandate for the change of leadership after the CA election. But against the people's expectation, his visit could hardly bring any significant change in the political standoff.

To some, the timing of his visit was not appropriate as India was hardly in a position to alter the course of political confrontation, There was a time when it facilitated the signing of 12-point Understanding by the Seven-Party-Alliance (SPA) and the Maoists, as the tyranny of monarchy then was their common enemy. After the first Constituent Assembly, the Maoist government led by its leader Prachanda resigned as his dismissal order of the then CoAS, Rookmangud Katwal, was overruled by the president. The Maoists held India responsible for obstructing their endeavour to capture state powers by removing the CaAS strategically. They took recourse to the old slogans related to nationalism, cancellation of 1950 treaty and declaration of Zone of Peace etc. raised by monarchy during Panchayat days to sideline the democratic forces and the people who were clamouring for democracy and equal rights. They did not hesitate in showing China card as well. Thus, they tried to exert political pressure on India on the one hand and sought dialogue with it, on the other, by placing India in a fix, as India wanted political leaders to act as per expediency.

Ironically, against the Maoist's call for the cancellation of the 1950 treaty, the Maoist insurgency proved its effectiveness of the treaty, which allowed the free movement of citizens of the each country in another's land, as the number of Nepalese people residing in India increased during the Maoist insurgency which forced most of them to cross over the border to save their lives along with young kids.

The second three-day (20-22, April, 2011) visit of SM Krishna to Nepal was confined to his meetings with the political dignitaries alone. The visit was different from the previous one because of change of guard in Nepal. Jhal Nath Khanal had replaced PM MK Nepal. There was no signing of any Memorandum of Understanding and no release of any joint statement. However, he laid the foundation stone of the integrated customs office at Birgunj. Of course, he could meet PM J N Khanal who keeping in line with the diplomatic tradition, expressed his desire to visit India first before embarking on his tour to Istanbul (May 9-13).Perhaps, the Nepalese foreign secretary was sent suddenly to India to chalk out the details of his visit, which sadly could not materialize. Interestingly, before the minister's visit commenced, Indian Foreign Secretary Nirupama Rao had visited Nepal in the last week of January 2011. She too had visited all those political personalities, whom SM Krishna met. Perhaps, the South Block was not satisfied with Rao's assessment, or she herself requested the minister to have his first-hand assessment of the political situation of Nepal.

Purpose of Krishna's Visit in Nepal:

Apparently, the main purpose of Krishna's visit was to have dialogue with the new establishment, as the chemistry of the government had drastically changed. In place of MK Nepal and his coalition partners, JN Khanal, who too was a CPN-UML leader, was heading the coalition with the UCPN-Maoist as the sole partner having the largest number of members in the CA. During his meeting with the PM Khanal, while extending invitation for India visit to the PM, he sought approval of the extradition treaty and check on the smuggling of fake Indian currency notes. He also raised the issue of showing black flag to Indian envoy. Moreover, the three-hour-long meeting with UCPN-Maoist chairman PK Dahal 'Prachanda' acquired significance. It was believed that the Indian diplomacy could not change the mindset of Prachanda towards India, but succeeded partially. The breakthrough was impossible since Prachanda was himself suffered from the Indian interference twice: first, while dismissing the former CoAS Katwal and secondly, in his failure to get himself elected as PM.

Two Decisions Taken:

Fortunately, Krishna's visit coincided with two major decisions taken by the two parties. First, the Nepali Congress had successfully patched up its long difference between NC president Sushil Koirala, and Sher Bahadur Deuba, leader of another NC faction, who once led the Nepali Congress (Democratic). And, secondly, 'Prachanda', had taken a 'U-turn' as he put forward his proposal for peace and new constitution against his earlier call for people's revolt in the context of the extended tenure of the CA ending just on 28 May, 2011.

Interestingly, Krishna's visit also invited a controversy over meeting CoAS Gurung, whom he had met last time too. The Indian foreign secretary too had met him during her last visit. He was reported to have advised all stakeholders to keep the army neutral and professional. His advice was taken unkindly by some quarters, as usual by raising questions like, was he right in meeting the CoAS? Had he gone out of his way in advising so? As per practice, the CoAS of each country is the honorary army chief of the other's.

Significant Outcome of Krishna's Visit:

Finally, the outcome of the visit seemed to be more than what met the eye. Krishna succeeded in convincing Prachanda to pave the way for Dr. Baburam Bhattarai to head the government, as Prachanda was himself a contender as per agreement between Khanal and Prachanda to head the government in turn. In reality, PM Khanal was proved ineffective as PM by the agitation of the NC and the prolonged election to choose his successor due to the neutrality of his party, the UML, in the voting, in which Prachanda was himself a candidate against Ram Chandra Paudel of the NC. Ultimately, Prachanda allowed Bhattarai to contest the election who became PM by winning election with support from Madhesi outfits in August 2011. The tenure of the CA was amended till it was fixed by the Supreme Court to last till 29 May, 2012. Unfortunately, the CA stood dissolved during the Battarai's regime without delivering any constitution.

India's new External Affairs Minister Salman Khurshid visited Nepal on 9 July, 2013. (3) Though the visit was hardly for nine hours, it stormed the almost calm political atmosphere whose dust took considerable time to settle down. During his visit, the Minister had hectic engagements. He visited his counterpart, Foreign Minister, Madhav Prasad Ghimire and discussed bilateral issues. He also made courtesy calls on the president and the Chairman of the Council of Ministers. Two letters were exchanged regarding India's logistic support for the security agencies and the Election Commission. A cheque of Rupees 800 millions covering the cost of 764 vehicles of different kinds was handed over to the government.

Unwarranted Controversy:

His visit was made when the chance of CA election to be held on 19 November, was looming large due to the constitutional and political challenges to be met in a limited time frame and the uncertainty over the participation of the 33-party forum led by the CPN (Maoist). Against this backdrop, the meetings that took place between some Nepalese leaders including some former Prime Ministers, Deputy Prime Ministers, and the visiting Indian dignitary in a hotel involving the issue of protocol status, attracted the attention of print and electronic media greatly. Against the international convention to hold the status of a former Prime Minister equal to that of a sitting cabinet minister rank and nothing more, the media ignorantly took the leaders to task for not adhering to the protocol. The status protocol is desirable in official meetings and events, but not in informal meetings. At times, the strict adherence to protocol may affect the bilateral relations, especially with regard to its own neighbours, which a nation cannot choose.

Purpose of Visit Evaluated:

Curiously, the purpose and effectiveness of the visit were marginalized, as it could have been evaluated in many ways. Was the visit required at all or not? Had it any thing to do with the visit of the Chinese State Councillor to Nepal last month? Was not the Indian ambassador enough to deliver the message of his government in unequivocal terms that it liked to see the next CA election to be held at any cost on the date announced earlier? The necessity of holding election was to bring stability, end lingering transition and adopt a people's constitution. Of course, all these were needed more for Nepal than its neighbours.

References:

1. The Himalyan Times, 6 July, 2005.
2. Ibid, art. SM Krishna's visit to Nepal, pub. in The Himalyan Times, 25/1/2010.
3. Ibid, art. Salman Khurshid's visit, pub. in The Homayan Times, on 22/7/2013.

❖ ❖ ❖

7

Chapter

PM Narendra Modi's Hegemonic Diplomacy

Three-Pronged Diplomacy:

PM Modi's diplomacy in Nepal can be divided into three parts. The first part covers the period (2014 to 2015) starting with his oath taking ceremony to the passing of the new constitution in Nepal and the economic blocake. The second part covers the period (2016 to 2018) after the blockade to the end of 2018. And the part-3 deals with regional diplomacy.

Part-1

Beginning of Diplomacy:

There has been a general complain of the Indian hegemonic attitude towards Nepal. Surprisingly, Narendra Damodardas Modi began a unique diplomacy, apparently in the form of hegemony, with his swearing in as the 15th Prime Minister of India on 26 May, 2014 after his unanimous election as the leader of the Parliamentary Party of the Bhartiya Janta Party (BJP), on 20 May. His election as PM was only a matter of formality as he was already designated much earlier as the prime ministerial candidate to spearhead the national election campaign. The oath-taking ceremony was unusually delayed for some reasons. It could have been caused for want of an auspicious moment to take the oath. Some serious issues like distribution of portfolios among the coalition allies and within its own party and also his personal involvement in the selection of his successor in his state of Gujarat. His decision to invite heads of the State and Governments of South Asian Association for Regional Cooperation (SAARC) would also have been one of the reasons for the delay as sufficient time had to be given to them for making arrangements for their visits.

Mini Delhi SAARC Summit:

The unusual invitation to the SAARC dignitaries by India requires evaluation. The visits of the SAARC leaders had definitely some positive and negative points. Positively, it could be named as mini or Informal Delhi SAARC Summit as all its leaders, except PM or President of Bangladesh had assembled there to interact with the new leader of India. No doubt, it had provided an opportunity for all leaders to know each other better. On the part of India, perhaps, PM Modi wanted to show the SAARC leaders how in a democracy, pluralism and unity in diversity could coexist, how Indian leaders could wear different dresses and speak in different languages on formal occasions too, as there was no regimentation regarding dresses and languages. Mr. Modi might have intended to have person-to-person contact with each leader and also have interest in acquainting himself with the bilateral problems, a member country had with India. Since he did not know the SAARC leaders well so far, as he was confined to his state alone, he would have availed of the opportunity for himself.

Negative Aspect of Meet:

Negatively, he failed to distinguish between domestic and external contexts of the event. The swearing in ceremony was not really a change of regime; it was rather only the transfer of power from one party to another and one coalition government to another. The same National Democratic Alliance (NDA) coalition had reoccupied the position, which it had enjoyed for six years only ten years ago. Of course, it has come with a clear majority in the House. It had lost the power unexpectedly in 2004 election and had failed to recover it even in 2009 election. Perhaps, this was the reason to celebrate the occasion with such grandeur.

Significantly, it seemed to overlook the position of most of the countries, which had constraint in bilateral relations with India. Some countries had to crack a hard nut before taking a final decision to accept the invitation. It might have put those countries in a fix to accept or reject the invitation outright. If it was accepted, it looked like just following the order, if rejected, it might have invited bitterness in the relation. To invite head of the states or governments at swearing ceremony and attending the ceremony are really too impractical to be practised. Actually all countries deserved thanks for having shown magnanimity in participating in the event. To consider the event academically in the context of Nepal, it would be better to elaborate it a bit.

The Psychology of Invitation:

Literarily, the word 'Invitation' means a spoken or written request to someone to do or go somewhere. Thus, any invitation has three factors. The first factor is the inviter, the second is the invitee, and the third one is the reason for invitation. It has two aspects, explicit and implicit. The main reason for invitation is always explicit but the implicit i.e. the psychology behind the act always remains hidden. Psychology, which indicates the mental set behind any work, can be known only in and through an analysis.

Man interacts with others while living in society. Hence, inviting someone or neighbour/s is a natural social phenomenon. One invites others for their participation in family and social functions.

In any act of invitation, the role played by the inviter is prominent as it is the inviter who initiates and invites anybody as per his actual need. It is commonly felt that only the rich and affluent people invite others so that their riches can be displayed. In contrast, the poor can hardly afford to invite others, as it will be like showing himself his poverty to others. An implicit factor is to show one's power and strength as well. A strong neighbour invites its weaker neighbour to show his might and also to exhibit its power which can be used in case of the weaker neighbour raised his head against him. Of course, in case of any national calamity, no invitation is sought, as it becomes the moral obligation of any country to share the grief of the suffering nations without any formality or reciprocity.

Obligation of Participation:

The position of the invitee is always secondary, as it has to respond to the invitation extended to it. Interestingly, any invitation from a superior or a stronger friend becomes an order or a compulsion. In the context of Nepal's PM being invited by India or China to attend their functions, has to be dealt in detail. Apparently, Nepal is being honoured, but in reality, it is asked to register its presence as a compulsion as and when these two neighbours want. Like India's invitation to Nepal, China has been inviting Nepal to attend its exhibitions' opening or closing ceremonies. And Nepal attends without asking for the presence of its counterparts from China.(1)

Message of PM Modi's Visit:

PM Narenra Modi's two-day visit to Kathmandu on the 3rd and 4th of August, 2014 had really created a state of euphoria. It was his first visit as Prime Minister but second in respect of number as he had visited Kathmandu a few years ago as well. Although, he was here virtually for about thirty hours, he utilized the opportunity by leaving lasting impressions of his personality on the common masses. He was perceived to have won the hearts and minds of the people as he tried his best to explain Indian stances on several crucial issues, which they had expected from him. By implication, he succeeded in erasing some misconceptions about his views on institutionalizing the achievements of the people's movement-2 and some long-standing controversial issues.

Explicit Message:

No visit was made without any purpose and therefore, it sent some messages both explicit and implicit. He delivered the explicit message himself through his address to the Constituent Assembly (CA). Accepting the gap of 17 years in the visits of two Indian heads of the government, he assured that it would not happen in the future. With his skill of oration, while touching upon the so-called controversial issues, he mesmerized all listeners including members of the CA/parliament. He dealt with the pseudo issue like the revision of the treaty of Peace and Friendship of 1950, the confirmation of Lumbini as the birth place of Buddha, sovereignty of Nepal, no interference by India, no receiving of power and water free of costs and offering cooperation in the development of Nepal. He admired the Maoists for discarding the politics of bullets and adopting the path of ballots as a means to social and political transformation. And politely he advised the members to complete the task of adopting the new constitution on time. He cautioned them to adopt a constitution to be accepted by all with a vision of a sage or saint (Rishimana) to avoid any confusion and conflict in the future.

Implicit Message:

The implicit message was that he was not prepared to address the political issues pending for years. It seemed that he, immediately after becoming Prime Minister of India in May 2014, had decided to offer prayers to Pasupatinath in Kathmandu on any Monday in the auspicious month of Shravan (between early July and early August). To actualize his dream, there were two alternatives before him: to request the Government of Nepal to make arrangement for his visit or to get invitation from it. He chose to invite the Nepalese PM first to get his invitation in return. Since to invite him alone at the earliest was not considered proper diplomatically, he, therefore, invited all the heads of the government/ state of the countries of SAARC region to attend his swearing-in ceremony. Sushil Koirala availed of the opportunity of visiting India. In return, he invited PM Modi to visit Nepal and he landed in Kathmandu on Sunday to offer his prayers on Monday.

Thus, the prime motive of his visit was religious; it was treated as political and special one, as his meetings with the president, leaders of all political parties and his address to the Constituent assembly were included in his itinerary.

Unprepared Diplomacy:

Finally, the visit appeared to be a sign of immature diplomacy. (2) It was really an unprepared visit, as there was hardly any proper diplomatic preparations in India due to lack of time on the part of officials or no mental preparedness of leadership to meet the challenges ahead as they failed to comprehend the situation prevailing in Nepal. Perhaps, PM Modi followed the same tactic of aggressive posture, which he had adopted during his election campaign in his country. The result was obvious. The draft for power trade agreement sent by Nepal in 2010 was overlooked and instead, a new draft of Agreement of Cooperation on power sector was sent to Nepal, which proved a red rag to the bull for Nepalese leaders. They vehemently opposed it. Foreign Minister Sushama Swaraj's visit to Nepal formalized the visit but failed to push ahead the thorny issues. She returned back with the first hand impressions from the horse's mouth by meeting all political leaders except the CPN-Maoist on the complex issues. As per her feedback on the sensitive points, PM Modi took up with them appropriately in his address to the CA cum Parliament subsequently.

During the visit, no agreement was signed on power trade and power development projects except modest agreements on the continuity of supplying iodized salt, cooperation between Doordarshan and Nepal Television. There was also an exchange of notes between the two governments to expedite preparation for the execution of Pancheshwar Multipurpose Project to be started within a year.(Sadly,the project report could not be finalized even during the two-day meeting on February, 27 and 28, ,2019.) The thirty-five-point joint communiqué was made exhaustive to include setting up a Boundary Working Group to address border disputes, etc. Since there was no spectacular achievement of the visit, PM Modi made his visit memorable and laudable by offering a soft loan of one billion US dollar to Nepal to be spent on developing infrastructures and hydropower as per its own priority, which confirmed his keen interest in the development of Nepal with an explicit message to the world over.

Second Visit for SAARC Summit:

He visited Kathmandu for the second time within four months to attend the 18th South Asian Association for Regional Cooperation (SAARC) submit held on 26th and 27th November 2014. Perhaps, knowing it well the date of SAARC summit, he had promised to visit Kathmandu breaking the gap of 17 years of previous regimes. He, thus, kept his word by coming over to Kathmandu showing himself different from his predecessors. Actually there was a gap of 12 years only as then PM AB Vajpayee, the first BJP Prime Minister had visited Nepal during the SAARC submit in 2002. He showed his shrewdness by not accepting the reality that there had been 23 times change of guard in Nepal during the last 24 years. (Since1990, the year of people's movement-1 to 2014).

Internal Political Condition:

Ironically, both his visits to Nepal had commenced when Nepal was in grip of serious political crisis as the process of framing a new constitution was stalled due to lack of consensus among the political parties. The politics was polarized in the CA on their well-defined stands. One group, which was led by the parties in power with nearly two-thirds majority in the House, wanted to adopt the constitution without taking any notice of the ethnic identities of the indigenous communities while carving out provinces in the process of state restructuring, on the one hand, and preferred to divide Madhes Pradesh (province) against the wishes of the Madhes-based parties, on the other. Another group, which was led by the UCPN-Maoist, had just opposite view, i.e, caste-based identities to be the basis of state restructuring and Madhes Pradesh to remain undivided.

Ambiguous Speeches:

His first speech, which he delivered in the CA, continued to echo in political circles till he delivered his second speech while inaugurating jointly by PM Sushil Koirala the Trauma Centre (built by India in 2008) on 25th November 2014. Interestingly, the major part of his previous speech in the CA was delivered in Hindi language. Apparently, some leaders failed to follow the contents of his speech properly or deliberately started distorting it to suit their stands in the CA. His counseling seemingly produced differing effects on the leaders. Some held that he was in favour of forming provinces not on the basis of north-south divide but on the basis of taking together all three geographic regions in all provinces. Naturally, they were very enthusiastic that his statement clearly showed a clear departure in India's stance of single Madhes issues. On the contrary, some leaders took it in a different way. (3)

Suggestions Misunderstood:

Similarly, it happened again when he spoke about framing the new constitution while addressing the Trauma Centre. In a very simple way, he advised the leaders to adopt a Constitution which could address the aspirations of all people-Madhesis, Paharis (people of Hill origin) and the Maoists too by making them feel their ownership of the new constitution to own it. Of course, he cautioned the leaders that if the new constitution did not come on time or was not adopted on time, it might create problems for the country. Some parties, who were dismayed by his previous expression, became happy that he had approved their views and vice versa. Some leaders went to the extent of calling it as interference in the internal matter of the country since drafting a constitution was an internal matter of the country.

His last visit appeared somewhat disgusting. First, his visit was marred by the cancellation of his visits to Janakpur, Lumbini and Muktinath, which he had committed during his last visit. Secondly, it seemed that he could not either understand the very psyche of the leaders here or take lessons from his Nepal's frequent visits with his candid expressions by confusing politics with diplomacy. (4)

Diplomacy of Action and Concern:

Undoubtedly, PM Modi was supposed to have acquainted himself with the political reality, especially with the intricacies of the demands made by the Madhesi community. The Community is the real link between the two countries through age-old open border dispensation. The community is having marital relations with the people of Bihar and Uttar Pradesh and has Maithili, Bhojpuri,

Abadhi as their mother tongues and Hindi as their common language. Though they have been living there even thousands of years before Nepal acquired its present geographic shape about two and half centuries ago, the ruling elite of Kathmandu never addressed their political aspirations. The issue of federation, which was incorporated in the Interim Constitution, 2007 by the Madhesi movement costing the lives of more than four dozen people, continued to linger. The first draft of the new constitution, which could not provide for proportional representations etc., provoked the Madhesi leaders to resort to protest and the protesters were fired upon indiscriminately. The number of killings rose to forty-eight.

New Constitution Adopted:

Despite the loss of precious lives, the main parties, the Nepali Congress, the CPN-UML and the CPN-Maoist adopted the new constitution without any detailed deliberation. The suppression of protesters by the security agencies compelled the protesters to block the main line of supply of materials from India to Nepal by staging sit-in protest on the Dashgaja (the ten-yard no man's land) between Raxaul and Birgunj and many other points too at the international border. However, some of them were withdrawn later. The responses from the people and the government of India were helpful.

Supply of Goods from India:

It was generally believed here that the Modi government might have restricted/blocked supplies of goods to Nepal for five reasons. First, the government did not defer the adoption of the new constitution to consider the demands of the disgruntled groups as suggested by India. Secondly, it helps directly the cause of Madhesi rights. Thirdly, it shows its displeasure on not declaring Nepal a Hindu state. Fourthly, it covers its long term planning to hold control over Nepal's water resources by forcing the present government to toe its line. And lastly, it wants Nepal to address its national interest including the security concerns in Nepal.

Consequences:

The scarcity of essential commodities made the lives of the common people in Kathmandu and hilly areas hard. However, the condition of the people in the southern plains of Madhes/Terai was in no way better, as they too faced the scarcity for about four months. It was almost a declared war of words between the governments of Nepal and India. The restricted supplies of goods including fuel from India was called by Nepal as an undeclared blockade by India. However, India termed it as an obstruction from the Nepalese side as Madhesi outfits had staged sit-in protests on several entry points including the main check post of Birgunj-Raxaul. The blockade forced Nepal to seek help from China, which was keen to support it. Nepal received a few tanker loads of petroleum products from China through a recently opened Kerung-Rasuagadhi route, which hardly mitigated the hardship of the people.

Part-2

Modi's Hectic Diplomacy:

The second part of his diplomacy commenced virtually with the visit of Indian president Pranab Mukherjee (5) who gave new impetus to the Indian diplomacy in Nepal by opening its jammed doors. India was interested in restoring its cordial relations with Nepal after the end of the undeclared economic blockade, which was started by Madhesi outfits in August 2015, and supported by India later. The relations deteriorated further when PM Oli had to resign in August 2016 paving the way for the new coalition government being led by SB Deuba of Nepali Congress. As a result, the visit of president Vidya Devi Bhandari to India was postponed abruptly.

It was believed that after a long persuasion by India, to restore the relations, the new government invited the president of India for a state visit.

Indian President's Visit to Nepal:

President Pranab Mukherjee, who was to retire after completing his five-year tenure, decided to visit Nepal. He completed his 3-day state visit to Nepal from November 2 to November 4, 2016 having very hectic schedule in Kathmandu covering Janakpur and Pokhara before flying back to India. During his one and half days stay in Kathmandu, he met not only his counter part but also the PM and senior leaders of the Nepali Congress, the major partner of the coalition government. He was particular in meeting with the senior leaders of the CPN-UML who are spearheading the anti-India stand believing Indian hand behind his ouster from power. He also met the prominent leaders of Madhes. He did not miss the opportunity of shaking hands with intellectuals and respectable citizens in the Indian embassy premise. He also participated in the seminar organized by India Foundation run by the RSS and other Nepalese organizations indicating India's interest in peaceful, stable and prosperous Nepal. Of course he expressed India's intention in harnessing water resources jointly and called upon Nepal to share the Indian' growth story'. He received the Honorary D.Litt. degree conferred upon him at the convocation ceremony by Kathmandu University where he expressed the stand of India on peace, stability and prosperity of Nepal and dwelt upon his own future plan of serving humanity after his retirement.

President Mukherjee's visit was to warm up Nepal-India relations, which were touching the lowest level in recent times. Since he had visited Nepal earlier as the Minister for Foreign Affairs of India, and had been the trouble-shooter of the Congress Party, the present establishment had chosen the very right person having acumen, experience and long association with the Nepalese leaders to untie the Gordian knot of present diplomatic confusion amidst Chinese aggressive financial involvement in Nepal limiting the Indian traditional leverage.

Different Perceptions:

The visit was viewed from different angles. To some, his visit was ill-timed as it seemed like interfering in the issue of amendment of the constitution, which was under consideration when the parties in power and the main opposition party the CPN-UML, which had been kicked out of the office, were at daggers drawn position. The section led by the UML was against the amendment and did not favour any consideration to the Madhesi demands and held India behind these demands fearing these demands might lead to the division of the country. On the contrary, the other section appreciated his visit, as it would facilitate the negotiation in favour of the agitating parties, since he was well known to the political leaders, who might lend their ears to his sound counsel. However, it was also believed that even if he did not pressurize the government, his presence in the capital itself was a message for the present establishment from New Delhi.

Prompt Visit of President of India:

Interestingly, after all, why did his government accept the invitation so promptly and fixed the schedule for visiting Kathmandu? To put it rightly, both sides were eager to improve relations at the earliest, which was marred by the cancellation of the visit of President Bidya Devi Bhandari to India by the then Oli-led government.

Significantly, he was the second president to visit Janakpur after N Sanjeeva Reddy had visited there. It was a religious place as well as the centre of Madhes politics. Curiously, no Indian Prime Minster could visit the place except PM Narendra Modi, who too could not visit Janakapur during his earlier visit to Nepal, as his programme was cancelled at the eleventh hour. Perhaps, there seemed to be a psychology behind restricting the visits of Indian leaders to Madhes region. In order to facilitate his visit to Janakpur, his visit to Pokhra might have been included in his itinerary. In Pokhra, he addressed the ex-Indian Gorkha army men at the pension center.

President Bhandari's India Visit:

It was Nepalese President Bidya Devi Bhandari, who went on her maiden 5-day state visit to India on 17 April 2017. (6) Her earlier visit was cancelled abruptly last year by the KP Sharma 'Oli' led government on account of alleged Indian involvement in his removal from prime ministership. President Bhandari, who was one of the vice-presidents of the CPN-UML before getting elected to the highest position in 2015, was a close associate of the party chief, Oli. The visit by a titular-head had impact to the extent it would be able to recoup ties after the cancellation of her last visit. Significantly, after the change of guard in Kathmandu, PM PK Dahal 'Prachanda' visited New Delhi, which paved the way for president Pranub Mukherjee's visit to Nepal. Diplomatically, India believes that the first foreign visit by any Nepalese head of state and government to India is a diplomatic achievement, which is a false notion as these visits have only cosmetic value.

Diplomacy of Congratulations:

It seemed that P M Modi was in hurry to open channels of diplomacy in Nepal. It was evident from his certain overtures to smoothen his relations with Nepalese leaders, as he congratulated SB Deuba on being elected as the next Prime Minster of Nepal, who was assuming power for the fourth time on 8 June, 2017 after a gap of 12 years. (7) PM Modi confirmed his telephonic call to Deuba in his tweet as well. Previously, Modi had also congratulated Deuba's predecessor PM PK Dahal 'Prachanda' earlier on 25 May2017 for his success in holding the first phase of local level elections held for 283 units in 34 districts of provinces no.3, 4 and 6 on 14 May, and hoped for Nepal's steadfast move on the path of political stability and prosperity. Interestingly, after majority of results of the first phase elections were published, Prachanda resigned on 24 May, 2017, from the post paving the way for SB Deuba, the leader of the largest party, the Nepali Congress in the House, to succeed him as per agreement reached between them while forming coalition. Was he congratulated for timely resigning from the post as anticipated by India?

It is usual to congratulate someone on any victory. However, it seemed unusual to congratulate a PM who had just completed the first phase of elections leaving behind more units to be elected. In phase two, elections were to be held for the rest 461 units in 41 districts of provinces no.1, 2,5 and 7, which were to be conducted on 14 June, were further rescheduled to 24 June had been once again extended to June, 28 on account of the month of Ramadan.

Curiously, it was difficult to understand whether PM Modi's thanks-giving formality to Prachanda was the execution of his government's 'Neighbour first' policy, or was it meant for bidding good bye to the outgoing PM or for appreciating his government for taking some crucial decisions like awarding contract for 1200-megawatt Budhigandaki storage project to China Gezhouba Group Corporation without any competitive international bidding, sanctioning Tarai fast track to the Nepal army, which was initially given to an Indian company and permitting China to study feasibility of railway track from Kerung(the Tibetan border point) to Kathmandu and to Lumbini finally.

These decisions did confirm that historically, Nepal was asserting its independence, sovereignty and self-respect. It had tried to move away from the India-dependent economy to China-dependent prosperity under the Belt and Road Initiative, the flagship of China' robust economy. It was an intriguing question too whether thanks were accorded to Prachanda for not completing election of second phase and not meeting the demands of Madhesi outfits for having proportional representation in the restructuring of the local level units that had been made the backbone of national administration and development.

Local Level Elections:

Interestingly, in the local elections, which were taking place after a gap of 20 years, the Madhes-based parties were demanding to amend the constitution and increase the number of local level units in proportion to the population of 20 districts of Madhes/Tarai. However, the Local Level Restructuring Committee (LLRC) fixed the number arbitrarily based on population up to 13,000, 22,000 and 40,000 respectively for the regions of High Mountain, Hill and Madhes for Village Councils, and 17,000, 31,000 and 60,000 for respective regions for Municipalities. It blatantly violated the right to equality as the citizens of Madhes were reduced to inferior citizenry to the people of hill and high mountain regions. It was not known whether PM Modi talked about the rightful claim of Madhesis or not while congratulating Prachanda and Deuba.

Hasty Diplomacy:

Again, due to some confusion, PM Modi showed his haste diplomacy by his early congratulations to the 'would be' PM of Nepal. (8) It was the breaking news in Kathmandu, as Radio Nepal, the government media, announced at 7 pm on 21 January, that Indian Prime Minister Narendra Modi had telephoned CPN-UML chairman KP Sharma Oli at about 4.30 pm wishing him a happy new year2018 and congratulated him as the future prime Minster. He enquired about the time to be taken for his formal election to the covetous post of prime minister. He also reiterated his standing invitation to him for visiting India at the earliest. In response, Chairman Oli too invited PM Modi to visit two religious places in Nepal-Janakpurdham and Muktinath, which were his cherished dreams. Coincidently perhaps, on 21 December 2017, exactly one month back, PM Modi had congratulated telephonically Chairman Oli for the grand success in parliamentary and provincial elections for scoring 80 seats against 165 seats (out of 275 total seats of the House of Representatives) under First-Past-the –Post system segment.

Curiously, it was too early to congratulate, as the final results by the Election Commission were still awaited. He had also invited Chairman Oli to India and had shown his eagerness to work with the new government. Of course, he had congratulated PM Deuba for completing the task of holding elections and also to Prachanda the coalition partner of the left alliance for faring well in the elections. Interestingly, PM Modi had confirmed having talked to the Nepalese leaders through his tweet message as well. However, this confirmation was missing this time, though the Indian Embassy had confirmed it.

Apparently, the subject matters of conversation, which were made public by the UML party secretary and the personal secretariat of Oli, were not of much significance. There was no point of extending New Years' greetings so late. Had PM Modi really intended to convey his new year's good wishes, he could have done it on 1 January, itself instead of 21 January. The expected time for forming the new government was well known to every one including the Indian Embassy, which might have updated its Ministry of External Affairs. Perhaps, PM Modi was very much interested in having personal rapprochement with the Nepalese leaders, which was appreciable. Similarly, the repeated invitation by PM Modi to Chairman Oli hardly carried much significance, as it was already extended to him during his earlier telephonic talk. It could also be interpreted differently as a satire on Chairman Oli as who would head the new government-Oli or Prachanda, was yet to be decided. And moreover, Prachanda might bargain like Shylock for the 'pound of flesh' mercilessly forcing the UML to lose significantly as it did not have majority of its own in the House of Representatives. Some considered it differently by way of strategic overture of PM Modi in a follow up move on the out of scene dialogue by the Indian establishment with the next leadership on the future relations with India. However, one could find only old faces of leadership except some changes in geopolitical conditions. Simultaneously, it was also felt that there was some confusion in India regarding the course of action to be taken decisively with regard to its relations with Nepal.

Diplomacy of Sushma Swaraj's Visit

The dust raised by the seventh visit of Indian External Affairs Minister Sushma Swaraj to Nepal could not settle down soon as dailies and weeklies carried different views on her two-day (February1-2, 2018) visit for many days. The visit, which was hardly for twenty-four hours, had really left many questions behind her. The minister herself told the media persons on her arrival at the Tribhuvan International airport that she had no specific agenda for the visit. However, Indian External Affairs Ministry officials claimed her visit as successful. In Kathmandu, her first engagement was with UML chairman Oli, which entailed that the main objective of the visit was to have direct communication with him. Of course, it was achieved with one to one talk and dinner along with several UML leaders.

An Uncalled for Visit:

Some were aghast at her visit, which was made before the new government was formed. Was this visit meant to facilitate Oli in occupying the highest executive post once again, which was snatched away from him in 2016, allegedly at the stance of India, or was it to boost the morale of Maoist Centre chairman Prachanda to continue his claim strongly for the post once again? It was also felt that her visit could have been made at a more opportune time by coming over here later, especially after the new government had assumed office so that she could have congratulated the new PM in person and extend the invitation to the Prime Minister personally. The visit appeared to have been made in haste. The aim of the visit was further questioned: was it really needed at all since PM Modi already had his telephonic talk with Chairman Oli? Had India wanted to communicate the change in its stand on the Nepalese constitution at the earliest without losing even a day for patching up its difference with Oli? Had India finally decided to alienate itself from Madhes on the constitutional amendment issue? Was PM Modi wrong in asking for an inclusive constitution? For the time being, though all such questions remained unanswered, the clear stance of the government of India over these issues would be known later.

Continuity of Conciliatory Endeavour:

Obviously, the visit was arranged in pursuance of the telephonic conversion PM Modi had with chairman KP Sharma 'Oli' on 21 January, 2018 last congratulating him as a 'would-be' prime Minister of Nepal and for the grand victory his party and the left alliance had secured in all three tiers of elections-local, provincial and federal. These elections were required to be conducted to implement the new constitution adopted in September2015 by the second Constituent Assembly, as the first had failed to pass it. While congratulating Chairman Oli, PM Modi had expressed his willingness to work with his new government and had invited 'Oli' to visit India. In response, Chairman Oli too had invited PM Modi to visit Nepal.

Interestingly, congratulations have been pouring in on Chairman Oli despite the final results of federal parliament were to be announced by the Election Commission as the results for 110 seats under proportional representation segment of 275 member-Lower House, was held up for ensuring thirty-three percent woman's representation in the House till election to the National Assembly (Upper House) was completed on 7 February, 2018.

Undoubtedly, the left alliance would form government at the centre along with six provinces, leaving one for Madhesis, with the massive mandate it had received. However skeptics viewed that the issue of leadership was to be decided by the alliance, though Oli had the genuine claimant for the post being the leader of the single largest party with more than double of the number of the members of the Maoist Centre in the House. However, it was being doubted that the lingering negotiation between Oli and Prachnada regarding the choice of leadership and the merger of these two parties that hanged in balance, which was announced on 3 October, 2017.

These two parties had seats sharing in the elections and were sharing different positions in provinces. Moreover, Prachanda seemed to be doubtful about the verbal commitment of Oli since he had betrayed Prachanda by not letting him succeed as PM in turn which was agreed upon by Oli while contesting election to PM's post with Sushil Koirala of the Nepali Congress with his support in 2015. Hence, Prachanda might have been seeking guarantee for a befitting post and reasonable share in the party and government.

Oli Ignored:

Curiously, during the last visit of Swaraj to Kathmandu on 11 August, 2018 for attending the 15th ministerial meeting of the Bay of Bengal Initiative for Multi-Sectoral Technical and Economic Cooperation (BIMSTEC), knowingly or unknowingly, she could meet all leaders except Oli. She did not speak any thing about him while addressing the civil society members and other important political invitees on the Embassy premises. However, she praised Prachanda for making room for PM Deuba and highlighted the coalition of the Nepali Congress and the Maoist Centre. There seemed some diplomatic lapses during her earlier visit.

Effect of Sushma's Visit:

Strikingly, despite several questions pertaining to her visit remained unanswered, the final results of her visit started coming in after a month when PM Oli government succeeded in getting supports from both Madhesi outfits, Sanghiya Samajvadi Forum-Nepal (SSNF) and the Rashriya Janta Party (RJP) while seeking the vote of confidence in the House of Representatives on 11 March, 2018. He got 208 votes against 60 out of 268 vote cast in the House. PM Oli had 121 votes from his own parties, 52 from the Maoist Centre and the 32 from Madhesi Parties and 3 from independents. PM Oli also negotiated with the SSFN and the RJP to join his government. However, the deal with SSFN, which was heading the coalition with RJP in province 2 (the Madhesis dominated province), was finalized and it joined the government. Though these parties were seeking a kind of guarantee from the PM on the issue of amending the constitution, the government had accepted their demands in a vague manner. The issue is still lingering.

Diplomacy of Pilgrimage:

It seemed that Indian PM Narendra Modi's pilgrimage to Janakapur, Muktinath and Pashupatinath was proved to be a blessing for him and his party, the Bhartiya Janta Party, which secured spectacular victory, not majority, in the crucial Assembly election held in Karnataka enhancing his personal popularity. The polling was held on 11 May, the day he embarked on his pilgrimage. His third two-day state-visit to Nepal (May11-12) had commenced from Janakapur, a

'Dhama' by landing there directly from India. Janakapur not only drew thousands of devotees every year from India on the birthday of Lord Rama and on 'Vivaha Panchami', the marriage day of Rama and Sita, but also provided impetus to political workers to fight for rights, which made it the centre of Madhes Movement forcing Kathmandu to declare Nepal a federal state. It has now become the capital of province no 2 waiting for the final approval of the provincial Assembly by two-thirds majority.

Modi's Visit to Janakapur:

Contextually, PM Modi wanted to visit Janakapur during his visit to Nepal in 2014, but it was cancelled at the eleventh hour. His long cherished wish to visit Janakapur, as a pilgrimage to offer prayers after assuming the office of Prime Minister of India, was fulfilled after almost four years through this visit. However, between 2014 and 2018, both Nepal and Janakapur were not the same, as these two had undergone sea change. Nepal was not the same what it was during his 2014 visit for several reasons. First, structurally Nepal was virtually a unitary democratic Republic not a duly elected federal state. Secondly, there was a devastating earthquake of April 2015, which killed about 9000 people and injures thousands and dismantled half a million houses. Thirdly, there was no new constitution duly adopted by the Constituent Assembly. Fourthly, there were no delineations for provinces formed at that time. Fifthly, there was no Madhesi led border blockade on India-Nepal border supported by India.

Similarly, Janakapur was no longer a place for pilgrimage alone. It had acquired its own political importance. It became the hot bed of revolution against the domination of Kathmandu and its elite over the marginalized and discriminated Madhesis. Province No 2 sacrificed the lives of more than fifty people against the discriminatory Constitution over and above the lives of more than fifty people which were sacrificed for making Madhes a province through the Madhes uprisings of 2007-8. It was not the same, as it became the capital of province No. 2, temporarily as the final decision on this score is yet to be taken by the Provincial Assembly.

Visits with Different Purposes:

Interestingly, the first visit of PM Modi was of religious nature as he had visited in the month of Shravana (July-August), which is regarded as an auspicious month for offering prayers to Lord Pasupatinath. However, it was turned into a political one, as he addressed the then Constituent Assembly. His second visit was related to the SAARC summit taken place in November 2014. His third visit was really a pilgrimage as he directly reached Janakapurdham and declared that he had landed there not as a PM but as a Prime Pilgrim.

Moreover, his visit was more than a pilgrimage was evident from some circumstantial configurations. In between his first and the third visit, some serious political developments had taken place that had significantly affected the Nepal-India relations. The new constitution was under deliberation in the Constituent Assembly (CA).

First Draft of Constitution Stirred Madhes:

In July/August 2015, the first draft of the constitution was made public, which was objected by the Madhesi parties leading to protests in which dozens of protestors were killed. Apparently, for pacifying the Nepalese Government, India sent its Foreign Secretary to Nepal to convince the then government to negotiate with the protestors, even by delaying the adoption of the constitution and which, however, proved fruitless. Protests and killing continued and ultimately, Madhesi outfits started sit-in protests at the Nepal-India border check points creating a border blockade. It continued for nearly five months giving immense hardships to the people and ultimately it was withdrawn. Nepal held India responsible for the blockade, as it did not want to give any importance to Madhesi protests, whereas India did not accept the allegation and held the blockade, as Madhesis - led. The episode soured the India-Nepal relations. Nepal rushed to China for urgent help and signed different protocols for trade and transit facilities.

Grant of One Billion Rupees:

Seemingly, his arrival at Janakapur directly was to show not only his personal religious sentiment but also of all Hindus of India towards Janakapur in particular and Madhes in general. His grant for one billion rupees to province-2 was just a friendly gesture towards Madhesis. It also replied to those in Nepal who opposed his visit in the past by finally visiting Janakapur in support of Madhes. He, thus, tried to please both the government and the Madhesis. However, he gave his visit a religious colour also by visiting Muktinath, where the Lord is worshiped through both Hindu and Buddhist traditions.

Ineffective Diplomacy:

An instance of an inapt diplomacy can be observed by the mishandling of a minor issue of shutting down a camp office of the Indian embassy in Nepal. The news of confirmation by the official spokesperson of the Ministry of External Affairs, government of India, on Monday (May 22, 2018) was almost heralded as a victory of nationalist forces of Nepal over India. He confirmed, "Government of India had already decided to wind up Camp Office and re-locate the personnel. This decision was conveyed by Prime Minister Modi to his Nepalese counterpart during his visit to Nepal last week." The closing of the field office of the Indian Embassy established at Biratnagar in eastern Nepal by India was the prominent main headline of all media on 23 May, highlighting the episode. Earlier, Prime Minister Oli announced at the first Parliamentary Party meeting of the newly formed the 'Communist Party of Nepal' on 19 May, 2018 that the field office of India at Biratnagar would be removed in the near future, as it had outlived its purposes. The meeting was held after the historic and long-awaited merger of the Communist Party of Nepal-UML and the Communist Party of Nepal-Maist Centre on 17 May. The crucial merger of the two parties took place after so many hiccups, though the proposed merger was announced on 3 October, 2017 itself.

Camp Office Needed Temporarily:

Interestingly, the field office was set up by India after Nepal had permitted it to open a temporary camp office in Sunsari District of eastern Nepal in2008 to issue passes to Nepalese vehicles to ply on Indian roads in the bordering regions after devastating Koshi river floods in 2008, which severely damaged a 17 km stretch of the East-West highway by changing its course. Previously, it was established in Sunsari district and was later shifted to a bigger town Biratnagar in the eastern part of Nepal.

The issue of winding up of the Indian office was raised many a times by Nepal in the past but to no avail. There are many questions to be answered. It can be viewed from different angles. First, why was the office not closed earlier? Second, had this decision been taken earlier, why was this not announced during PM Modi Visit to Nepal or immediately thereafter? And thirdly, has this decision been taken only in response to the PM Oli's patriotic decision?

Decision Delayed:

Undoubtedly, there was a long delay on the part of India in taking decision on closing down the office. It had enough time at its disposal to take the final decision as the repairing work of the damaged part of the Highway was completed within 3 years. There seemed some lapses in the comments of the spokesperson that the decision was communicated to the Nepalese Prime Minster by PM Modi during his two-day visit (11-12 May as pilgrim of Janakapur, Muktinath and Pashupatinath. The matter was so much important for the public of Nepal that it could have been announced publicly, not simply conveyed to the PM of Nepal. Had this decision taken earlier of PM Modi visit to Nepal, it could have been announced by the External Affairs Ministry itself as Nepal had repeatedly drawn India's attention to this problem. Apparently, the decision was not taken by the government of India till the visit of Nepalese PM KP. Sharma Oli to India in April last, when he was believed to have raised this issue with PM Modi in one-to-one parley. There was one more pertinent question to be replied, did India wait for the announcement by PM Oli asking the government of India to remove its office at the earliest to make him only the national hero with patriotism?

Closure of Office Made an Issue:

Curiously, it was believed that the temporary Indian office, which issued passes to Nepalese vehicles for plying on Indian roads outliving the utility after the damaged portion of the highway was repaired, was relocated to Biratnagar by Indian side unilaterally. After realizing the fact that the propose of the office was already fulfilled, the then Nepalese Foreign Minister Narayan Kaji Shrestha had taken up the issue through diplomatic correspondence with India to close the office. It was learnt that the Indian side, not only ignored the repeated drawing attention by Nepal on the one hand, but also lobbied with a section of the political leadership of Nepal to upgrade the facility into a consulate, on the other. It began engaging in various activities including scholarship distributions and even in gathering intelligence. As the facility was widely seen as infringing on Nepal's sovereignty, the then Dr. Baburam's Government in 2011 forwarded two diplomatic notes to New Delhi seeking removal of the facility. In early 2018, there was a bomb explosion near the wall of the building of the office. Some persons were arrested and the investigation was carried on. However, it was certain that the element, which was not happy with the Indian presence in Biratnagar, had exploded the bomb to send signal of warning to India to leave Biratnagar at the earliest.

Was It a Diplomatic Victory?

To get popularity, the former foreign minister and spokesperson of the newly formed party, the Communist Party of Nepal, Narayan Kaji Shrestha said that the removal of the office was the historic victory for a patriotic stand and he also congratulated PM Oli through twitter over the matter.

To sum up, it is difficult to hold whether India s succeeded in its diplomacy to extend its temporary office in Nepal for some extra period, or failed in its diplomacy by closing the office.

Part-3

Regional Diplomacy -SAARC and BIMSTEC

There are two major regional fora, SAARC and BIMSTEC, which provide opportunity for open diplomacy. In the context of South Asian Association for Regional Cooperation (SAARC), its two-day successful celebrations of the 18th summit had ended with 36-point Kathmandu Declaration on the 27th November, 2014. The meet was really concluded gracefully with the hand shaking by PM Narendra Modi and PM Nawaz Sharif with special initiative of PM Sushil Koirala who rightly expressed satisfaction over the success of the meet, which ended with the seemingly reduction of the bitterness between India and Pakistan.

Most of the previous agreements related to trade remained more or less unexecuted. They got stuck when the tern of Pakistan came. It was commonly felt that SAARC had been made hostage of India-Pakistan relations, which in return moved round the issue of Jammu and Kashmir. Had this issue been settled, there would be no place for the army to play in Pakistan, which had been in power most of the time since its formation. No third party could come forward to mediate since it was an internal problem of Pakistan. Ironically, the two major parties-the Pakistan Peoples Party and the Muslim League led by Nawaz Sharif, which are always draggers drawn at each other, indirectly allow the army to rule the country.

Perhaps, since Pakistan failed to counter India in SAARC, it wanted support from China, its all-time friend. Previously, it might have prompted Nepal to ask for Chinese membership to get its support. In just concluded summit, the leader of the Chinese delegation stressing its geographic proximity with SAARC with sharing of borders with its five countries, had shown interest in deepening integration, elevating its relation and also seeking mode of help in promoting peace and development in the region. Although he did not come out directly seeking its membership, his interest was obviously in its upgradation from mere observership. Interestingly, bilaterally it is involved vitally in all countries of the region. It has substantial financial involvement in the development projects of Sri Lanka, Maldives. It is a serious partner of Pakistan in many fields including atomic energy. With India, it has a good business relationships. In Afghanistan it is investing heavily in mining sectors etc.

Regional Conditions:

Curiously, the political conditions, which were prevalent at the time of formation of SAARC, had undergone one specific change. There is only one difference that the cold war, which once used to dominate the world politics, does not exist now. Most of the nations under SAARC including Nepal were allergic towards India and were once under American and Chinese axis. Quoting Gen. Ershad, Jawed Naqvi, a Delhi-based correspondent of Pakistan's Dawn daily rightly summarized the motive behind the formation, "Saarc began as a childish prank to corner the big boy in the neighbourhood, Gen. Ziaur Rahman who conceived it and Gen. Hossein Mohammed Ershad who hosted the first meeting in Dhaka both bore a baffling grudge against India. 'We were all allergic to India in South Asia, so we decided to join hands to deal with the problem together,' were the words of Ershad, who said in a TV interview a decade after flagging off the seven-nation club in 1985. During his interview, he described, "Gen. Ziaul Haq, president Junius Jayawardene, president Maumon Abdul Ghayoom and king Birenra who joined him at the inaugural session as the dramatis personae who were as fitted nicely the description of political allergens and allergies." He adds further, "Remarkably, India's detractors had another thing in common. They were all traditionally at ease with the United States and China. That is how the diplomatic cookie crumbled in South Asia during much of the Cold war. " (9)

Genesis of SAARC Formation:

Significantly, SAARC was formed only when it was decided that no bilateral issues would be discussed in it. India was aware of the intention of its neighbours. So after a long persuasion, under the leadership of Rajiv Gandhi, India agreed to participate in the formation a regional organization. Indira Gandhi was always reluctant to form such organization, as she knew that the entire surrounding was under the domination of the Western block and China. Rajiv Gandhi, who on account of his mother's assassination, took the reign of the country suddenly, turning himself from a pilot to a PM, was young and almost novice to politics. However, facing the challenges of his new assignment, he took some bold steps in domestic and international spheres. He signed pact with the Akali leader Harchand Singh Longowal to meet their demands. He signed pact with the agitating Assam Gana Prishad Chief, Kumar Prafulla Mohanta, to settle the Assam issues. On external front, he saved Maldives from the hands of some hired armed men to capture it. Similarly, after signing accord with Sri Lanka for devolution of power to Tamils, he sent Peace Keeping Force there to disarm the Tamil Rebels. Of course, he could save himself from the baton charge on his head from a guard during guard of honour in Colombo but could not survive the assassination plot of LTTE.

To make SAARC effective, the role of PM Narenda Modi could have been different. He could have shown his saintly mind (rishimana) in meeting all heads of state/government, especially of Pakistan, at least in return to show magnanimity to them who were present at the time of his oath taking ceremony some six months ago. He could have been spectacular in showing diplomacy with his Pakistan's counterpart, who might have his own domestic compulsions in cross- border firing and meeting the Kashmiri separatists. The suspension of Secretary level dialogue could not have remained stalled for a long time. The democratic forces in Pakistan could have been strengthened by India as democratic Pakistan could only solve the Kashmir issue and other bilateral problems. It could have also provided much-needed impetus to SAARC.(10)

SAARC Yatra of Indian Foreign Secretary:

Indian Foreign Secretary Dr. Subramanyam Jaishankar's visit to Nepal, as claimed, was under his SAARC Yatra (SY), i.e. travel to the nations of SAARC. He had embarked on SY during early March 2015. He visited Bhutan on 1 March, Bangladesh on 2 March, Pakistan on 3 March and Afghanistan on 4 March. Interestingly, he stayed hardly for 24 hours in these countries, in contrast with his stay in Nepal for a longer period keeping in view his country's involvement in various fields. Curiously, after visiting four countries, he winded up his SY only to resume it to cover Nepal almost after a gap of one month.

Subramanyam's Stay in Nepal:

He resumed his two-day hectic visit to Kathmandu on 2 and 3 April, 2015. He met all those who were involved in constitution making including CA chairman, Subhash Chandra Nembang, Pushpa Kamal Dahal, PM Shushil Koirala, KP Sharma Oli, and president Dr. Rambaran Yadav. He also met Foreign Minister Mahendra Bahadur Panday and his Nepalese counterpart, Shankar Bairagi and discussed about the timely implementation of bilateral projects. He also sought Nepal's support for India's candidature for permanent seat in UN Security Council and also for non-permanent seat for 2021-22. The calling off the proposed nation-wide general strike on 2 April, by the 30-party alliance led by the UCPN-Maoist made his visit successful as he could convey the message that India was for early constitution promulgation with all stakeholders on board to institutionalize the achievements of the peace process.

Analysis of Resumption of Visit:

Did Nepal not deserve India's priority in its foreign policy? Or did it require special attention of the highest-level diplomat, which was not possible in continuation of his SY in March itself? Was SY country specific or SAARC centric or both? Had his visit to Nepal been delayed in anticipation of ending of the continued deadlock in writing of the new constitution before it actually took place? In the context of ongoing inconclusive dialogue between the leaders, his visit was seen differently. One section viewed his visit fruitful, while others considered his advice as interfering in the internal matter of Nepal, which had been the bone of contention in Nepal-India relations. The earlier view held India's role as significant in getting 12-point Understanding signed by the Maoists and the seven-party alliance in November, 2005, which resulted in epochal changes that had taken place in Nepal. Yet to some, his visit was SAARC centric by and large.

Broadly, the very name of his visit as 'SAARC Yatra', though appeared inappropriate and concealing, yet had significance. It seemed inappropriate because it hardly suited the foreign secretary level official visits to SAARC countries. It appeared to be concealing, as it had been intentionally used to hide the very diplomatic compulsion for the visit of Indian foreign secretary to Pakistan by making it a part of his series of visits to different nations under SY that covered the visit to Pakistan. It was an unpleasant situation on the part of India to send its Foreign Secretary to Pakistan to resume the dialogue cancelled unilaterally by it earlier just to show a tough posture on dealings with separatists in Jammu and Kashmir (J&K), which turned out different from the stand taken by the previous government.

India for Resumption of Dialogue:

Diplomatically, India seemed to be under pressure to resume the stalled Secretary level regular dialogue cancelled by it on 18 August, which was to be held on 25 August, the date agreed upon by the then Foreign Secretary Sujata Singh on 23 July, 2014. The meet was cancelled only four days ahead as Pakistan's ambassador to India, Abdul Basit met some J&K leaders on 18 August. Hence, it was the responsibility of India to resume the dialogue with Pakistan. To avoid this embarrassing situation, PM Modi adopted indirect channel of communication like expressing telephonically his good wishes to PM Nawaz Sharif for the cricket team of Pakistan in the coming Cricket World Cup and informed him of the next visit by the Foreign Secretary to start dialogue with Pakistan again. Therefore, Jaishankar's visit was indirectly Pakistan centric and not SAARC or Nepal-centric.

Indian Regional Diplomatic Leadership:

The second regional forum is BIMSTEC, a sub-regional organization with seven members-Bangladesh, Bhutan, India, Myanmar, Nepal, Sri Lanka, and Thailand. Initially, it was called BIST-EC as it was formed by Bangladesh, India, Sri Lanka, and Thailand through the Bangkok declaration on 6 June, 1997. It was renamed as BIMST-EC when Myanmar joined the block on 22 December, 1997 at the ministerial meeting held in Bangkok. It was rechristened BIMSTEC when Nepal and Bhutan joined the organization in February 2004 at the 6th ministerial meeting hosted by Thailand. It seems that the formation of the regional block was planned to link the countries situated on the bay of Bengal with sea navigation facilities under India's 'Look East' policy and presently under 'Act East' policy. The inclusion of Nepal and Bhutan was in the interest of India which wanted to form a separate regional subgroup to effect connectivity.

It was started in 1997 with six sectors-trade, technology, energy, transport, tourism and fisheries as its objectives to be attained by sharing and accelerating growth through co-operation in the areas of common interests using regional resources and geographical advantages. Now the areas of common interests have increased to 16 by adding Blue Economy and Mountain Economy in addition to Agriculture, Climate Change, Culture, Counter Terrorism and Transnational Crimes, Energy, Environment and Disaster Management, Fisheries, People-to-People Contact, Poverty Alleviation, Public Health, Technology, Trade and Investment, Transport and Communication and Tourism.

Kathmandu Meet Not Properly Represented:

Its 15th ministerial level meeting was held on 11 August, 2017 in Kathmandu with the decision to conclude Free Trade Agreement and Grid Interconnection at the earliest. (11) The Indian External Affairs Minister, Sushma Swaraj and junior foreign ministers, of Thailand, Myanmar attended the meet. The then Prime Minister Sher Bahadur Deuba, while inaugurating the ministerial meet, hoped that the meet would endorse the regional cooperation framework on trade, investment and connectivity. He stressed that in this age of globalization and economic interdependence, regional cooperation was not a choice but compulsion. He, thus, called upon the member states "BIMSTEC to give due attention to the different needs of its members in order to be effective as a regional grouping."

Nepal Chairing BIMSTEC AND SAARC:

As per the scheduled 19th SAARC summit was to be held in Pakistan on 9 and 10 November, 2016, Pakistan would have chaired SAARC. But the summit was cancelled as India and some other nations refused to participate in the meet. Though Nepal is negotiating with the member countries, it is still uncertain when the next submit will take place. In view of the continued strained India-Pakistan relations, Kathmandu's limited economic and diplomatic resources handicapped its maneuvering capacity in steering SAARC.

Ineffectiveness of SAARC:

Ironically, India, despite being the main initiator and major stakeholder, could not come up with success. India seemed to fail in providing leadership, as it was skeptic about the formation and role of SAARC from the very beginning, as most of its members were more or less in the Western block, which was hostile to India. Its performance was affected by intermittent ups and downs in Pakistan-India relations. Critics hold that SAARC was a non-starter as it was made the hostage of India-Pakistan relations. Sri Lanka and Bangladesh could not remain unaffected by the cold war syndrome. Even after the restoration of democracy in Bangladesh, there were changes of government with every five years. Nepal too was not happy with India. Monarchy was not ready to part with its sovereignty. It wanted unqualified support from India. Later on, India's stand underwent change to support the democratic aspirations of the people, which annoyed the monarchy.

To get rid of the neighborhood hostility, especially to keep Pakistan out of the conglomeration, and in accordance with India's 'Look East' policy adopted by the then PM PV Narsingha Rao, the concept of a sub-regional cooperation was mooted. However, not to displease Pakistan, its boundary of south Asia was extended to the east by including two ASEAN nations, Thailand and Myanmar making BIMSTEC possible. Unfortunately, BIMSTEC with its two decades of history too could not come up to the expectations of the member states.

India's Failure in Directing SAARC & BIMSTEC:

Unfortunately, SAARC and BIMSTEC have remained by and large rudderless, as their natural initiator India was unable to give direction to them. It might be for two reasons. First, it took much time to record fast economic growth to rebuild its economy to provide economic support to its neighbours who were actually in need. Secondly, the internal political compulsions and personality clashes were also responsible for its poor performances. It seems that there was no Indian policy, only parties' policy, as one party was ready to undo what earlier regime had done.

Interestingly, during the early days of SAARC, any serious reader would recollect the assertion of the then Sri Lankan President Jayawardene at the 3rd SAARC Summit held in Kathmandu in 1987 that the fate of South Asian region was safe under the leadership of Rajiv Gandhi, the then PM of India. With its rapid economic growth, India's policy of 'look East' got impetus under Narshimha

Rao. Though Dr. Manmohan Singh tried to improve India's relations with Bangladesh, the Teesta water sharing agreement was opposed by one party, which was led by Mamta Banerjee, the Chief Minster of West Bengal and the passing of the Land Boundary agreement obstructed by another major party, the B.J.P. tarnished the image of India, of course, in the interest of the B.J.P which got it through when came to power. Further, PM Modi's criticism of previous Indian PMs for not visiting Nepal during the last 17 years, during his address to the Nepalese parliament was appreciated as if he were not the part and parcel of the Indian establishment. All these prove that the domestic interests prevail in deciding Indian diplomacy by and large.

Weak Diplomacy in BIMSTEC:

PM Modi made his 4th visit to Nepal to participate in the 4th BIMSTEC summit held in Kathmandu, on 30 and 31 August 2018. During the summit, he showed his profound inclination to play a greater role in strengthening the grouping in the days to come. He offered 34 scholarships to researchers, students and professors of the group at North-Eastern Space Applications Centre and 30 scholarships in Nalanda University and 12 research fellowships at Jawaharlal Institute of post-graduate Medical Education and Research. A Centre for Bay of Bengal Studies will also be established at Nalanda University. He also intimated that BIMSTEC members would be engaged at least till 2020, beginning with India Mobile Congress in coming October. He was ready to host BIMSTEC Start-up Conclave to engage entrepreneurs of the region. In the same year, India is hosting International Buddhist Conclave. He was interested in organizing other events like, BIMSTEC Youth Summit, Youth Water Sports Event, Band Festival and Second Disaster Management Exercises. Significantly, he did not forget to invite all member countries to participate in the events.

Overshowing Led to Strategic Failure:

Curiously, PM Modi's intention to play a greater role in BIMSTEC during his speech sent two massages. First, he was really interested in making the organization vibrant despite its slow pace. Secondly, he gave the list of events to show as if he were in election mode distributing sops to the voters. The organization is supposed to be cared by all member states and not to be dominated by one country. Sadly, his open invitation to all member states to participate in the BIMSTEC military drill culminated in a political row in Nepal.

The event was to be organized in Poone (India) from September 10 to September 16, 2018 (for six days) was made an political issue in Nepal, as it withdrew its participation in the event. Joint military drills were arranged by different armies with a strategy in view, where as governments considered it politically. The event was being arranged in consultations with all stakeholders of all member states and preparation and participation were going on smoothly. A team of the Nepal army had reached there to make arrangements of the event. The new CoAS was ready to leave for Poone as per schedule. But it suddenly took a political turn and Nepal withdrew from its participation holding that BIMSTEC was not a military set-up. Significantly, Thailand too joined the event as an observer.

References:

1. Mishra, Birendra Prasad, art. Psychology of Invitation, Republica, 24/6/2014.
2. Ibid, art. Modi's visit to Nepal, THT, 12/8/2014.
3. Ibid, art. Mixed bag, pub. in Republica, on 21/10. 2014)
4. Ibid, art. Modi's visits to Nepal, THT, 2/12/2014.
5. Ibid, art. Outcome of the President's visit, pub. in The Statesman, 7/11/2016
6. Ibid, art. Relevance of Bhandari 's India Visit, pub. in The Statesman, 18/4/2017.

7. Ibid, art. Not much to cheer for Modi in Nepal ties, pub. on The Statesman, 5/6/2017.
8. Ibid, Another Pakistan in Nepal, The Statesman, 17/8/2017
9. The Kathmandu Post, dated November 27, 2014
10. Mishra, Birendra Prasad, Long Shadows, Republica, on 10/12/2014.
11. Mishra, Birendra Prasad, art. Region needs more from India The Statesman, 17/8/2017.

❖ ❖ ❖

8

Chapter

Counter Diplomacy of China and Pakistan

Counter Diplomacy Through Elections:

Against the Indian haste overtures to bridge the gap of understanding between the two governments, its diplomacy was being checkmated by China and Pakistan. The successful elections to local levels units paved the way for simultaneous elections to Provincial Assemblies and the federal Parliament. The first phase of election was held on 26 November, for 37 parliamentary seats and 74 assembly seats in 32 districts under First-Past-the-Post electoral system and the second phase election for 128 parliamentary and 256 assembly seats in 45 districts were held on December 7, 2017 leaving 110 representatives to be elected under Proportional Representation system.

Uniquely, only two major alliances had dominated the electoral scenario. The first was the communist alliance constituted by the Communist Parties of Nepal, including, the UML and the Maoist Centre, which was still a partner of the ruling coalition government led by the NC, the other alliance. Some fringe Communist Parties too had joined the left alliance, which was fighting election on the plank of nationality, sovereignty, independence, self-respect, stability and prosperity. It supported the constitution as it was. Its slogans had anti-Indian intonation. The second was democratic alliance led by the NC, which headed the government. Parties under this alliance were two Rastriya Prajatantra Parties supporting constitutional monarchy and were against secularism. The plank of this alliance was to save the present democratic achievements and make the constitution acceptable to others by amending it to meet their aspirations. It advocated that the authoritarian regime of the communists would obstruct the all-round development of individuals and the country.

Strategically, the formation of left alliance was announced on 3 October, 2017 Strategically almost after completion of the third phase of local level elections in September and also after the announcement of the dates for federal and provincial assemblies by the government. The Naya Shakti Party-Nepal (NSPN) led by Dr. Baburam Bhattarai, ex PM and one of the founders of the Communist Party of Nepal-Maoist, which had joined the alliance initially, finally severed its relations within ten days of its formation to contest election on its own symbol. Curiously, the Maoist Centre was continuing in the government despite its ministers had been deprived of their portfolios. The House stood dissolved on 15 October 2017, as per provision of the constitution.

Left Alliance:

There were two pertinent questions being raised in political circles in the context of the formation of the left alliance. First, how did Prachanda and Oli come to terms to form an alliance when they were at daggers drawn with regard to power sharing previously? Secondly, were these two coalitions able to sweep the election results with two-thirds majority or comfortable majority to have a stable course?

Seemingly, frenzied consultations were made under pressure to meet some internal and external designs. Prachanda, on 7 October,

2017, accepted to forge an alliance with the UML in haste due to 'extreme pressure and compulsion' without any further clarification during the politburo meeting and political training of the party. To some, forming a single party after the election was really a distant goal, but contesting the elections was just half the way of replacing the Deuba government before the elections. However, the left alliance parties had their own goalposts. The MC, which could not fare well in the previous elections, decided to join the alliance for getting benefit from the elections and to secure Prachanda's victory to ensure his crucial role in the future. Some reasons for the UML 's initiative to form an alliance were quite obvious. First, it would head the alliance. Secondly, the ego of its chairman would be satisfied with Prachanda's coming ultimately to work with him. Thirdly, it would receive MC's support in local level units. And lastly, it would help secure majority in the elections.

Significantly, it was also presumed that China had been steering the whole exercise as a common commander since it was not satisfied with the dismantling of the pro-China UML and MC coalition government a year ago. It might have planned to replace the anti-China stance of the NC led government, which, perhaps, collapsed due to some internal constraints of the parties, and limited time to execute it due to the elections. Finally, the alliance proved effective as CPN-UML became the single largest party and Maoist Centre acquired the third position. The seats of these parties almost secured two-thirds majority in the House.

Purpose of Pakistan PM's Visit:

The visit of Pakistan Prime Minister Shahid Khaqan Abbasi to Kathmandu (March 5-6, 2018) was viewed in different contexts including the earlier visit of Sushama Swaraj, Minister for External Affairs of India, as its rippling effect continued for a long time. (1) Nepal seemed to have down played the visit very tactfully by announcing the date of the visit - only two days ahead of the visit to show it a normal visit to congratulate the newly appointed PM KP Sharma Oli, who had taken the oath of office on 15 February, 2018. Of course, it was not an ordinary visit as the visit had regional dimensions. It was questioned: had PM Abbasi been so keen to congratulate PM Oli in person he could have visited Nepal earlier? And was it necessary to congratulate PM Oli when he was already congratulated?

Discussion about SAARC:

It was feared that once Nepal, which was being conceived as a transit nation between two economic neighbouring giants, China and India, might not become a battlefield for these two nations for securing unqualified support from it. The visit by the Prime Minister of a SAARC member country was taken in all seriousness by completing all paraphernalia by the government. Nepal, as the chairman of this regional block, not only welcomed him but also listened to him with attention, as it had to act upon. Pakistan, which was to host the 19th SAARC summit and to take the charge of SAARC as the next chairman in 2016, could not succeed in holding the summit as India declined to participate in the meet on the ground of an attack by Pakistan at its army base in Uri sector of Jammu and Kashmir. Some other regional countries including Nepal backed India. Against this backdrop, it was natural for Pakistan to get the process restarted as early as possible that remained stalled so far. Its desired to host the next summit was confirmed by Bishnu Rimal, Chief advisor to PM Oli, who said, "Both the leaders have agreed to sort out issues through mutual consultations if any dispute arises in the SAARC process". It was a challenge for Nepalese diplomacy to have negotiation with India and Pakistan to find out a way to restart the process, as a new stable government was in place in Nepal after ending the period of political transition. Nepal seemed to be in a position to influence India to come to negotiation table, as India had to listen to Nepal in present geopolitical competitive context.

Neutralizing Swaraj's Visit:

The visit acquired more significance, as it followed the Indian Minister for External Affairs Sushma Swaraj's two-day visit to Nepal (February2-3). Curiously, these two visits contrasted each other, as Indian Minister Swaraj visited before PM Oli took the oath of office and PM Abbasi came after twenty days of PM Oli's swearing in ceremony. It was presumed that PM Abbasi visit had been planned with a view to neutralizing Swaraj' influence, if any at all, on the new Nepalese establishment.

On Behalf of China:

Perhaps, the PM Abbasi's visit was hardly an urgent national need for Pakistan, as it had been facing its internal political turmoil. It might have been planned to kill two birds with one stone.

On the one hand, since it was fade up with Indian stand on no negotiation with it, Pakistan is interested in having a substitute by forming another political and economic block with China and Nepal to ignore the importance of India in Nepal, on the other. He might have visited Nepal as per Chinese advice to gauge the effects of Swaraj's visit to Nepal, especially with regard to Chinese Belt and Road Initiative (BRI), of which Nepal is also a signatory. Despite China's repeated reminders, Nepal had been allegedly delaying in providing details of the projects to China, which it wanted to construct under BRI on priority basis. The visit might have been arranged to convince Nepal if it had any doubt about the economic effect of BRI. Notwithstanding the demerits, Pakistan might have highlighted the benefits of China Pakistan Economic Corridor (CPEC) as well. He might have suggested similar economic corridor for Nepal too. Significantly, the Pakistan Embassy in Nepal was engaged in presenting the benefits, which Pakistan had been deriving under CPEC, to different groups of Nepalese intelligentsia.

Interestingly, the Visit of PM Abbasi could also be looked into in the context of Indian PM Modi's congratulations to PM Oli. The Indian PM had congratulated him twice before his appointment and once after assuming the office. Indian Minister Swaraj, during her visit to Nepal, had her first engagement in Kathmandu with UML chairman Oli to have direct communication with him. Significantly, the outcomes of foreign dignitaries' visit to Nepal would be known in due course.

PM Oli's Cosmetic Delhi Visit

The real outcome of the second three-day state-visit to India (April 6-9, 2018) of P M. KP Sharma Oli was finally known by his visit to China in June. (2) However, PM Oli diplomatically claimed his visit successful and fruitful at the airport while talking to the media persons by referring to the point 2 of the joint statement issued in Delhi.

"The two prime ministers resolved to work together to take bilateral relation to a newer height on the basis of equality, mutual trust, respect and benefit." Perhaps, the inclusion of these terms like equality, mutual trust and respect in the joint communique made him hold his head high as he had assured the parliament before embarking on India visit in his usual nationalistic rhetoric.

"There will be no agreements that go against national interests like sovereignty, nationalism and lowering down our heads disgracing our country". Significantly, despite Foreign Minister Pradeep Kumar Gyawali's assertion that no new agreements would be signed, and the implementation of the previous agreements would only be specifically emphasized, the three new agreements signed during the visit added a feather in Oli's cap.

Apparently, the visit itself did not take the Nepal-India relations to a new height but actually sought commitment of both sides to reach it. Of course, the visit was, indeed, a step towards removing misunderstanding and building mutual trust, as both sides avoided to discuss the points of disagreement and deliberately did not include several crucial issues in the communiqué. In contrast to his last so-called successful six-day (February 18-24, 2016) state visit to India, which had ended without any joint statement, the latest visit was better. The visit succeeded in opening the door of opportunity. However, Modi's no proper reply to the queries raised by him regarding the delays in implementing earlier agreements and completing the projects under construction, created doubts that the agreements signed previously and the projects under construction had hardly drawn India's proper attention.

PM Oli's China Visit for Cementing Relations:

Interestingly, his visit had commenced when he had two strong wickets in hand. First, he was there within two months of his assuming office with the backing of a massive public mandate his left alliance (formal unification not duly declared) has secured nearly two-thirds majority in parliament and had spectacular victories in Local level and provincial elections. Secondly, he had firm commitment from China for its full financial support under the Belt and Road Initiative to develop infrastructure, which Nepal had been craving for.

The complexities of Nepal-India relations are inherent in psychological perception and physical or geographic situation. First, India, being a democratic nation, extended its helpful hand to the cause of establishing and flourishing of democracy in Nepal and landed itself in a marshland. Secondly, the diplomatic perspectives of both countries always remained ambiguous. The latest visit of PM Oli reflected it glaringly. It seemed as if there were no misunderstanding and if there was any real misunderstanding at all, it was painted as resolved diplomatically. Thirdly, though India is on three sides of Nepal and China is on the north, China has been playing a critical role in Nepal shaping indirectly its relations with India. These two seem to have been competing with each other for bringing Nepal under their influence for their strategic interests. And lastly, it is the geographic situation of Nepal and India, which was determined by the Himalayas, has made their destiny common since thousands of years ago. The relations based on natural resources ever remained undermined and ignored, resulted in creating confusion in Nepal-India relations.

The commencement of his second visit to China, for which Foreign Minister Gyawali left earlier for setting grounds, would actually make the final result of his India visit known to all. PM Oli had played his card well by visiting India first in line with old practice. This satisfied the traditional ego of India, which believed its superiority to another country that the new prime minister visited India first. All knew it that he continued to attach more importance to China than India. He had made several commitments to China during his last visit when Nepal's relations with India were at their lowest point. It was to be seen as to how he cared for their concerns, as strong relations needed taking serious note of each other's vital concerns.

Preparing Ground for PM Oli's China Visit:

Nepalese Foreign Minister Pradeep Gyawali had planned to leave for China earlier before PM Oli visited India, which was really hastened. Naturally, his visit was delayed, as he had to accompany his PM. Minister Gyawali, who was on his first official visit to China after assuming the office of foreign minister, met Chinese vice-president Wang Qishanhis and Foreign Minister Wang Yi on 18 April, 2018 and had joint press conference with his counterpart.

Significantly, Gyawali, whose China visit had commenced within ten days of the completion of the PM KP Sharma Oli's three-day state visit to India (April 6-8, 2018), had accompanied the PM as the FM. It indicated the urgency of the visit that both Nepal and China had realized. Foreign minister's visit was planned well before PM Oli's visit to India for two reasons.

First, PM Oli did not want to waste even a single day in finalizing development projects and fields of cooperation under Belt and Road Initiatives (BRI) that Nepal had already signed.

Secondly, PM Oli had to take China into confidence as early as possible about its deliberations and commitments he would make to India regarding Nepal-India mutual relations and also about India' stance on Chinese involvement in Nepal.

Perhaps, the present establishment of Nepal did not believe in India's commitment offer for development as many projects that were funded by India had not progressed satisfactorily. Of course, India alone could not be blamed. Moreover, during India's Madhesi led blockade of 2015,which was second in number, as the first one had taken place about three decades ago, China came forward to help Nepal by sending a few dozen petrol and diesel tankers to Nepal to meet the requirements of Kathmandu valley. The poor connectivity between Nepal and China came in way of getting sufficient and regular supply.

FM Gyawali's China visit paved the way for a successful PM Oli's visit to China, as he would concentrate on closing deals of cooperation in the fields of transport connectivity, agriculture, industries, technology, human resources, natural resources, environment, trade and investment. There seemed to be hardly any field that had been left out. Now, Nepal had to incline entirely towards China for its development.

With regard to the projects to be identified under BRI, some of them were decided during the PM 's visit but certainly some projects would be decided to be given to China during Chinese president Xi jinping's visit which would commence after Nepalese president Bidya Devi Bhandari visits China in April to participate in the second International Belt and Road Initiarive in Beijing, which will be presided over by Chinese president Xi Jinping. Durin her visit, the much awaited Agreement on Transit and Transportation will be formally signed with some corrections to the taxt sined in September, 2018. Interestingly, the original text was signed almost three years ago during PM Oli 's first visit to China. Significantly, the protocol will allow Nepal to use four sea ports and three lant ports of China for third-country trade in the near future. (3)Most probably, China may take up the job of improving the poor infrastructure in Nepal, especially, the Rasuwagadhi transit point.

It is interesting to note the candid remarks by FM Gyawali on the proposed railway link from China to Nepal that he made regarding his dream to travel from Nepal to China in a modern train. It seemed it would be actualized soon in contrast to his any previous experience of traveling by train in India. His wish really symbolized the inspiration of those who might be fading up with India. However, against his wish, it was no wonder, that he might have to travel to Delhi by India made railway coach that might not be so comfortable as Chinese coaches would be.

PM Oli's Second Visit to China Successful:

PM Oli completed his six-day (18 to 23 June 2018) official second landmark visit to China, which was keenly awaited with its much significance. It was his second visit during his two tenures in two years, as he was there in March 2016 earlier. His meetings with President Xi Jimping and his counterpart Li Keqiang were very cordial. He succeeded in deepening ties with the top leadership, exploring new areas of cooperation and signing new agreements based on 10 points of agreement reached during his earlier visit. He looked for Chinese support in three areas, direct aid, and cooperation and joint investments. As scheduled, new agreements were signed for energy, power transmission, railway connectivity, post-earthquake reconstruction and border entry points. Nepal had proposed the following projects to China:

Under transmission lines, it had named six projects-Galchhi-Kerung cross-border line, Butwal-Attariya-Mahendranagar line, East-West line, Marsyangdi-Kathmandu line, Kosi and Karnali corridors, Doublecitcuit transmission line around the Ring Road. Under Hydropower sector-Kimathanka-Aruna, Tamor, Sunkosi 11 and 111, Narsingh Gad and Uttarganga. Under water resources-Panchkhal Lift Irrigation project, Sunkosi Main Diversion Multipurpose project, Eastern Tarai river management, Mid-hill Tar Lift Irrigation, Groundwater feasibility for Chandragiri buried valley and Mahadevakhola rainwater harvesting project.

Nepal-China Friendship Tested:

Significantly, the signing of accord to develop a cross-border railway line connecting the Tibetan town Kerung with Kathmandu for railway connectivity was heralded as the most signicant initiative in the history of bilateral cooperation. Interestingly, senior officials from both sides signed 14 MoUs and letters of exchange, which were followed by nine agreements by Nepalese and Chinese public and private sector companies. The major agreements include - Investment board Nepal and Huaxin Cement Company of China to develop a Rs 15 billion Huaxin Narayani Cement; Butwal Power Company and Sichuan Investment Group to work together on Marsyangdi Cascade to produce 1000 megawatt electricity; Nepal Electricity Authority and China's State Grid Corporation will construct a 159-km Kerung-Galchhi transmission line. It is held that a strong infrastructure of cross-border power connectivity will link Nepal in the regional power grid that already encompasses China, Thailand, Myanmar, Laos and Cambodia. Curiously, the MoU on railway project made a strong commitment towards its timely completion. It was due to a great degree of technical details involved in such a huge infrastructure project, which demands massive engineering works. FM Gyawali told the reporters that the Detailed Project Report of Kerung-Kathmandu railway would be completed in another one and a half years and the project would be completed in additional five years. Both sides took the railway project as the standout achievement of the current visit. It was also agreed upon to encourage Nepalese and Chinese airlines to operate additional direct flights between the two countries. However, it was not clear whether the Chinese assisted projects would fall under BRI or not, the two sides agreed to intensify implementation of the MoU on Cooperation under the BRI to enhance the connectivity. Attracting more Chinese tourists to Nepal was given due importance. On international diplomacy, they agreed to strengthen cooperation in the UN and other multilateral fora. They also agreed to enhance coordination and cooperation within the Shanghai Cooperation Organization, SAARC, and other regional cooperation mechanism.

The apparent outcome of his visit confirmed that China was its real well-wisher and a viable partner in Nepal's development. It gave impetus to China that Nepal is no longer an India-locked country. PM Oli succeeded in showing the world in general and India in particular that China was a country to rely upon. Materially, it is still to be seen as how China comes with a broad heart to help Nepal without putting it in its debt trap.

References:

1. Mishra, Birendra Prasad, art. Thank you for coming, pub. in The Kathmandu Post, 16/3/2018.

2. Mishra, Birendra Prasad, art. To newer heights, pub. in The Kathmandu Post, 9/4/2018.
3. The Kathmandu Post, News-After 'minor' corrections, Nepal and China allset to sign transit protocol, 2/3/2019.

❖ ❖ ❖

9

Chapter

The Formal Diplomacy

The overall diplomacy of a country is the joint product of the decisions taken by the government of the state (foreign ministry) and their efficient execution by the representative (the ambassador) in the country where he is assigned to discharge his duties. Moreover, the feedback of the diplomat forms the very basis of the diplomacy the country decides to adopt apart from the requirements of national and international obligations.

Nepal and India who are geographically and culturally intertwined have a common destiny as both are struggling to raise the standard of living of their masses, of course, with different political structures at times have hardly common approach to the problems faced by them separately. Politically, Nepal and India stood on similar footing as India got freedom from the British rule in 1947 and Nepal threw the oligarchic Rana rule in early 1951. With the political setup changed in both countries by mid-twentieth century, India enjoined more or less an established democracy and Nepal continued to starve, by and large, of the fruits of democracy, their economies too needed supplement their sustainable economic development.

There is a common conception that the Indian diplomacy in Nepal has not only been ineffective but has failed considerably. As a matter of fact, there was hardly any diplomatic approach between Nepal and India as senior Nepalese political leaders and even the late kings had personal relations with the political leaders of independent India. On account of personal relations, perhaps, two bigger river projects were signed during the period of MP Koirala and BP Koirala's prime ministerships, when King Mahendra was at the helm of affairs and were executed later.

Limited Role of Ambassadors:

The role of ambassadors was limited in Nepal as it was under direct control of PM Nehru who always kept the Ministry of External Affairs under him officiating as the Foreign Minister. Nepal perhaps, occupied the topmost priority of India for four reasons.

First, Nepal, which was only a northern neighbour, suddenly became the buffer state between India and China after China took over of Tibet that shook the Indian traditional perception of insurmountability of its northern frontier.

Secondly, Indian leaders were confident of the commitment of the Nepalese leaders for the Indian concern about its security as some of them were well known to them and some had participated even in the Indian independence movement. Thirdly, it accepted Nepal's full independence. And lastly, it facilitated Nepal to usher in a democratic era by acquiring the real power from the Rana oligarchy by restoring the real monarchy with a commitment to frame people's constitution through the elected Constituent Assembly to establish real democracy. It, of course, proved to be a political blunder later since it displeased almost all stakeholders as they wanted to use state power unhindered finding India as an obstacle.

Post-Independent Indian Ambassadors to Nepal:

India has appointed about two dozen ambassadors to Nepal since independence. The names of the Ambassadors are: 1. Surjit Singh Majithia (1947-1949), 2. CPN Singh (1949-1952), 3. B. K

Gokhale (Oct.1952- Dec.1954), 4. Bhagwan Sahay (1954-1959), 5. Harishwar Dayal (1.2.1960-19.05.1964), 6. Shriman Narayan (20.11.1964-17.12.1967), 7. Raj Bahadur (05.01.1967-22.01 1971), 8. L P Singh (22.01.1971-05.09.1973), 9. Maharajakrishna Rasgotra (08/12.1973-17.10.1976), 10.N B Menon (21.11.1976-31.03.79),, 11.N P Jain (30.06.1079-28.07.1982), 12.H C Sarin (31.01.1983-31.01.1986), 13. A R Deo (24.12.1986-31.12.1989), 14. Lf Gen. (Retd) S K Sinha (20.02.1990-02.01.1991), 15. K V Rajan (15.03.1995-13.06.2000), 16. Dev Mukharji (14.06.2000-30.11.2001), 17.Dr, I P Singh (01.12,2001-17.05.2002), 18. Shyam Saran (31.10.2002-25.07.2004), 19. Shiva Shankar Mukherjee (06.10.2004-23.04.2008), 20. Rakesh Sood (25.04.2008-11.08.2011), 21. Jayant Prasad (25.08.2011-25.08.2011), and 22. Ranjit Rae (02.09.2013-28,02.2017).

Roles Played by the Ambassadors:

The first Indian ambassador to Nepal was Surjeet Singh Majithia. His role in making spadework for drafting of the constitution of 1950 by Indian constitutional experts was not insignificant in any way. The Indian diplomacy was at the very beginning stage during his tenure. C.P.N Singh, is remembered as the ambassador who played the crucial role in overthrowing the Rana regime by helping King Tribhuvan to take shelter in the Indian embassy. However, Ram Hari Joshi a Nepali Congress leader and a former minister mentions in his autobiography that in 1951 when there was first coalition government in Nepal and Ganeshman Singh was a minister, the Indian envoy had requested him to get some fish from a pond at Balaju to serve in the dinner of some Indian guests in the embassy as he could not receive fish from Patna. Singh was hesitant as he used to feed the fish himself every morning.(1) B.K. Gokhale, who succeeded Singh facilitated in signing the Treaty Of Extradition between India and Nepal on 2nd October, 1953, by him forte Government of India and Matrika Prasad Koirala for the Government of Nepal.

Rasgotra who joined the Indian Embassy as second secretary in April 1954 narrates the condition of diplomacy in Nepal. In his words:

Ambassador Gokhale said: "The embassy had no information at all about what is happening in the country beyond the valley of Kathmandu, and because of acute shortage of personnel, we know little even about going-on in the valley's political circles, whose numbers and activities had multiplied manifold after the end of Rana rule. Access to those circles would no problem but it required a degree of finesse and sophistication in enhancing routine contacts into friendship for India." (2)

Nepal was passing through a difficult transition from autocratic rule to democratic governance and it needed all kinds of help from India. He writes:

"Managing that change in the nature and scope of India-Nepal relations was not going to be easy. For while Nepal was in dire need of reviving and reorganizing its military, economy and administration,which were destroyed by the widespread armed insurrection triggered by King Tribhvan's voluntary exile, India ran the risk of getting too deeply in the process and attracting criticism and accusations of interfering in Nepal,"(3)

After the demise of King Tribhuvan in 1955 in Switzerland, Bhagwan Sahay was a member of the high-powered Indian delegation, led by Vice President Dr. S. Radhakrishnan, to witness the coronation ceremony and facilitate the young king Mahendra on his coronation on 2 May, 1956. A few months later King Mahendra paid his first state visit to India for nearly two weeks. During his tenure, a library-cum cultural centre was established in Kathmandu. Cultural shows by way of arranging musical concerts were arranged on regular basis on two occasions for celebrating the independence and republic days. During Harishwar Dayal's tenure, the elected government of the Nepali Congress led by BP Koirala was dismissed, parliament was dissolved and all political activities were banned and the constitution was suspended.

A Breakthrough in Nepal-India Relations:

Sriman Narayan was the sixth ambassador to Nepal. During his tenure, the Arms Assistance Agreement was reached on 30 January 1965 very secretly. The people knew it after a long time when Rishikesh Shaha found a copy of the agreement in a British library. The agreement was confirmed vide the letter written by Yadu Nath Khanal, Royal Nepalese Ambassador to Y.D. Gundevia, Foreign Secretary to the Government of India, New Delhi. Raj Bahadur, a former minister of Indira Gandhi's cabinet, was appointed Indian ambassador to Nepal to play his political role. He negotiated successfully with the king to make him allow a senior military officer in the embassy and have exchange of information about the developments harmful to both countries. It is believed that his role in getting BP Koirala and other leaders released from jail was significant.

M Rasgotra came to Kathmandu again after a gap of seventeen years as an ambassador to Nepal. After the presentation of his credentials, he had to face officially inspired anti-Indianism when the then PM Nagendra Prasad Rijal and Foreign Minister Gyanendra Bahadur Karki complained him about the slow progress of the India-aided development projects as Chinese projects. After making personal inspection to the projects, he found everything normal and gave all relevant facts and figures not only to the Foreign Ministry and other offices but also to the media but they ignored them as they were influenced by the Chinese embassy. Rasgotra writes in this connection:

"Mr Prime Minister, India itself is a developing country with many needs and insufficient resources; its aid projects in Nepal, undertaken at your government's request, involve a considerable sacrifice of the needs of our own people. If you are not satisfied with our aid, I shall immediately stop work on the projects and send the Indian personnel back to India. You can hand the projects over to China. Derogatory treatment of India, inspired by Nepalese officials or by a foreign embassy in Nepal is not acceptable." (4)

As per practice, royal family used to visit Indian embassy. Rasgotra, taking advantage of his early personal relations with the the king and the queen, invited them to private dinners in the premises of the embassy, which was utilized to convince the king to give proper treatment of ex-PM BP Koirala and bring him back to Nepal. He also narrates as to how he convinces Koirala' sister to persuade him to come to Nepal.(5) He also cited an example of state sponsored protest over Sikkim integration to India in April. During the course of protest, Indian embassy was almost under seize and effigies of Nehru and Mahatma Gandhi were brunt. His lodging four-point strong protest with the Foreign Minister and informing the king of the government of India to recall its ambassador in protest for the time being had its effect on the Nepalese government. He writes:-

"Action by the Nepal Government to meet our demands was shift. A public apology was voiced on three occasions by Prime Minister Rijal; he also paid a day's visit to Delhi as a conciliatory gesture." (6)

N.B. Menon was appointed during the emergency by Indira Gandhi and he continued till Janta Party government signed two agreements with Nepal. N. P. Jain succeeded Menon and remained in office till Indira Gandhi regained power. H.C. Sarin was appointed during Indira Gandhi's second inning. He was sent to

Nepal to deal with carefully, as he was a very seasoned bureaucrat having Gandhi's confidence. During A. R. Deo's period, there was economic blockade by India on the issue of Nepalese demand for separate trade and transit treaties.

After the first people's movement of 1990, new government was elected in 1991 under the new constitution of 1990. Ambassador Sinha'a role was not of much diplomatic significance, though he provided Indian support for the general election. India helped the Election Commission to complete its job by providing some logistic support like providing ballot boxes and indelible ink etc.

Prof. Bimal Prasad played a somewhat more political role than diplomatic. Most of his time was spent in his effort in keeping the ruling Nepali Congress intact as it was a house divided against itself. He used to shuttle between PM GP Koirala and his opponent Ganeshman Singh and former PM KP Bhattarai. It seems that since there was some indirect role of India in the People's Movement –2, it thought its duty to help smooth functioning of the elected government after three decades. The Indian diplomacy was so apparent that the behaviour of the ambassador very often was disgusting. Even the signing of 12-point Understanding in India is not digestible to some.

Critical Period of Diplomacy:

Interestingly, K.V. Rajan stayed here for the longest period of more than five years. This was the period when governments changed very often. The mid-term poll delivered a hung parliament and the first left government took the office on 1 December 1994 but could last hardly for nine months. There was, series of unstable governments during his tenure. Dev Mukharji witnessed the most tumultuous condition of Nepal as King Birendra and his families were assassinated on 1 June, 2001 and Gyanendra ascended to the throne.

There was hardly any role to be played by him. Dr. I P Singh came to Nepal at very critical juncture. The state of emergency was imposed to deploy the royal army against the Maoist insurgency. S. B Deuba dissolved the Lower House as his party was against the imposition of the emergency. The Congress party was divided, which affected the democratic setup greatly. Any significant diplomatic role played by him remained unnoticed.

The role of Shyama Sharan was a bit different. Perhaps, the perception of India had undergone a drastic change in looking at Kathmandu as Nepal. In accordance with the agreement between the two prime ministers, the government of India in consultation with the Government of Nepal started investing money on developmental works in Tarai, especially on constructing buildings for schools. In the words of Saran:

"As ambassador, I tried to make a start by connecting with the Madhesis through small community-level development projects and by regularly visiting the Terai to directly meet their local leaders. This was done without reducing in any way the number of community projects we had in the hill areas. It was obvious that the development projects promoted by the Nepali government and even by many of the international and western aid agencies were almost entirely focused on these areas. The Terai plains were completely neglected until the Indian embassy began some community projects there."(7) It was the time when CPN-Maoist leaders had contact with the office of PM AB Vajapayee. Significantly, Saran, as the Foreign Secretary of India, had accompanied Dr. Karan Singh who visited Nepal during the second People's Movement of 2006. It is believed that he was in Kathmandu to persuade the then king Gyanendra to surrender the state power to the people. He claims that he persuaded the then CoAS Pyar Jung Thapa not to go for suppressing the public uprising and making it easy for the peaceful transition of power. (8) Perhaps, all area commanders of the army had advised the king not to suppress the agitation, as the issue was to be negotiated with political stakeholders.

His successor Shiva Shankar Mukherjee was the second long residing Indian ambassador who was here for four years. It was the period when the second people's movement with support from the Maoists threw the autocratic rule of the king and the dissolved parliament was restored. During his period, the twelve-point Understanding between the Seven Part Alliance under the leadership of GP Koirala and the Maoist president PK Dahal 'Prachnda' was signed in Delhi on 22 November, 2005 laying the foundation of the People's Movement of 2006. Significantly, Shyam Sharan was the foreign secretary of India then. Rakesh Sood succeeded him as the twentieth ambassador. During his tenure, the first Constituent Assembly (CA) election was held and Pushpa Kamal Dahal 'Prachanda' led CPN-Maoist government was formed. The episode of dismissal of the then CoAS Katwal was significant as his dimissal order was overruled by the president Dr. Rambaran Yadav led to the resignation of Prachanda. It is believed that he played a crucial/effective role in the overruling of the dismissal order. Jayant Prasad who succeeded him played a significant role in making the sitting Chief Justice Khil Raj Regmi as the Chairman of the Council of Ministers to hold the second CA election as a neutral government.

Ranjit Rae was the 12th ambassador to Nepal. The new constitution was to be adopted during his period. He had to face many challenges, as all major parties were adamant to adopt the constitution without addressing the demands of Madhes - based parties, on the one hand, and Madhesi outfits were agitating in the streets facing bullets of the security agencies. Ultimately, Madhsis and Rashtriya Prajatantra party voted against the adoption of the constitution that was passed with a big margin. The Madhesi agitation was being suppressed very high-handedly thorough bullets that resulted in the 'sit-in' protests on several Indian border checkpoints, which blocked the supplies from India with assistance from the Indian people and the government. M.S.Puri is the incumbent ambassador, whose diplomatic performances are yet to be observed. However,he seems to follow the footsteps of his External Affairs Minister and the Prime Minister by pleasing PM Oli as his first visit was to meet him.

Media/Publicity for Diplomacy:

Interestingly, during the last six decades, India and Indian diplomacy could not get support from media in Kathmandu. In the beginning, there was only one Nepali language newspaper - 'Gorkhapatra' which was owned by the state, and was naturally the mouthpiece of the government The english daily' The Rising Nepal' was owned by the government was started some time later. Radio Nepal was established in 1951, which too was state-owned, These media were just reporting the news provided by the government. With the change of the regime, from autocratic rule to democratic system, some dailies and weeklies started getting published. Significantly, some of them seemed to be India - friendly as they used to support Indian stands on different issues. However, these papers either did not have mass circulation or no circulations at all. Most probably, these were published to show that these are published for record sake. After the people's movement of 1990, some dailies and weeklies came up with mass circulation, as these were critical of the government. The number of dailies has markedly increased in recent years.

Publicity never seemed to capture the attention of the embassy. The embassy did not seem to be serious about its publicity. Of course, it started printing a magazine of its own named "Bharat Samachar" which continued for some years and was stopped long ago. The reason for Indian embassy not taking interest in local publicity was that almost all major Indian English and Hindi dailies and weeklies were available in Kathmandu which quenched the intellectual thirst of the people. Moreover, India and the Indian embassy, perhaps, did not take interest in local publicity also because they always felt their dominance in both political and economical spheres.

Questionable Role of Diplomats:

The overall diplomacy of a country is a joint venture of the decisions taken by the minister and his ministry meeting the requirements of national and international obligations and also on the basis of the feedback of the diplomat (the ambassador or minister) together with his action. Significantly, students, who go to India in hundreds, come back to Nepal after becoming anti-India. Ambassadors' subjective decisions on rewarding fellowships too proved ineffective. The Indian bureaucracy does not seem to bother about the final outcome of the aid given to Nepal.

Scholarships:

During the Panchayat regime, students were sent to the then USSR for their education. Many of them, if not all, returned to their native land after becoming communist. Of course, their number was limited. Just contrary to it, students, who went in hundreds to India for education, came back to Nepal after becoming anti-India and hardly India-friendly. The story continues even today. The government of India or the Indian bureaucracy does not seem to bother about the political aim of the aid given to Nepal It never looked into its usefulness and its fallout on the recipients of education in India at the cost of Indian expenses. It was like pouring water on the sand.

References:

1. Joshi, Ramhari, Atma Katha Tatha Nepali Congressanga Gansiyaka Samjhanaharu, p. 139.

2. Rasagotra, pp, 96, pp 2016,
3. Ibid, pp-94-5
4. Ibid, p-300)
5. Ibid. pp-301, and 308-9
6. Ibid. pp-302-307
7. Saran Shyam, How India Sees The World p-170-1, 2017.
8. Saran Shyam, Ibid.

❖ ❖ ❖

10

Chapter

Conclusions

During the last seven decades, India seems to have faced three categories of Nepalese establishments in Kathmandu. The first category of governments was of benign nature. They were neutral and to some extent favourable to it. The second type of governments were strategically hostile to continue anti-India activities without displeasing India, as Nepal was dependent on it for the supplies of essential goods and military hardwares. And the government of third kind had been out and out hostile to it. These three types of establishments correspond with the three phases of political events and development that took place during this period.

Diplomacy has limited role to play, as it is an instrument to achieve the goal of foreign policy. Hence, the sole objective of a diplomat is to execute the decision of the country s/he represents through one's ability of negotiation and dealing. To a great extent, bilateral relations between two countries are dependent on psychological, social, cultural, economic, and geographic conditions of the countries.

The Indian diplomacy in Nepal had been challenging and continues to be so with a greater degree. One of the reasons is the psychology of dependence, on the one hand, and forgetting reciprocity, on the other. It expects some thing without paying any thing in return. Its one-sided approach appears to be a common psychology.

Rationale Behind Psychology:

This psychology has its reasons. First, the lack of bureaucracy, at the early stage, was the main reason that made it rely on India for its support. Previously, there was no permanent administrative setup in the country till 1950, as it was governed by the whims of the highest authority. The immediate job of the new government, which took over in 1951, was to create a permanent service mechanism to deliver services to the people in the changed democratic dispensation. There was hardly any permanent staff, as every year there used be 'Pajani' in which some administrative staff had to be dismissed. Hence, it needed administrative and logistic support from India, which was the only neighbour to come to help in no time to meet its requirements. Secondly, it depended on India for political support as well, as it was not stable politically. Thirdly, even for economic development, it had to lean on India primarily. India, which was itself in its formative stage, was experiencing difficulties in meeting its own developmental challenges with its limited resources. In fact, it was not in a position to meet all requirements of Nepal and naturally Nepal had to look beyond India. Its contact with the other nations enlarged its horizon to look beyond India politically and its exposures to the external world made it to interact and establish relations with the countries all over the world, which still continues.

India's diplomacy has been facing constant dilemmas in Nepal on several fronts. First, its foreign policy confronts with contradictions. The post-independent India decided to have a foreign policy that recognized and respected the sovereignty, integrity and independence of Nepal, on their one hand and wanted to have common foreign and defence policies, on the other. Ironically, the British India, which did not face any serious external challenge from China due to conditions of its own and that of the world, tried to meet the Chinese challenges very shrewdly. The post-independent India' s diplomacy in Nepal faced a new reality, at least psychologically, in the form of the forthcoming threat from China as it became the next-door neighbour by bringing Tibet under its control. The British succeeded in having greater control over Nepal only after 1816 when Sugauli Treaty was ratified by Nepal. Its relations with Tibet were somewhat defined in course of time but its relations with China was not defined then properly. There was no clearcut line of demarcation of border between India and China as the British got the border line, known as McMahon line, drawn only on the map, which was drawn by Lieutenant-Colonel Sir Henry McMahon. It later created border disputes between India and China.

The second dilemma is related to its special relation with Nepal. If its international borders with Nepal are restricted, it cannot boast about having special relations with Nepal and if borders remain open, though it can claim to have special relations, it needs continuous vigilance at the borders to check that no criminals and terrorists enter its territories to create havoc inside the country warranting constant security alert.

Simultaneously, the Kathmandu elite is adamant to have the open border restricted, if not sealed for it holds open border dispensation responsible for the imaginary flux of Indian immigrants to Nepal to upset the demography of Nepal. It has been pressurizing India directly and indirectly to control the movement of the people from India. Politically, with the eradication of malaria from the Terai region and deforestation, the people of hills and mountains were encouraged to settle in Terai to outnumber the original Madhesi inhabitants. For this purpose, the government decided to rehabilitate people from Hills to Terai, though in the name of landless people, established special Rehabilitation Company. Ironically, powerful people acquired enough land in Terai. As a result, the far-east and far-west regions of the country acquired the dominance of hill origin people over the Tharus in the west and the Satars in the east. The demographic situation got changed in favour of the hill-origin people increasing their decisive say on the national politics, on the one hand and reducing, if not eliminating altogether, the influence of the original inhabitants, on the other.

Its third dilemma is related to its genuine concern of security on its northern borders. To have its northern border secured, it always considered seriously holding Nepal under its security umbrella. However, after 1950, the Nepal-India relations through the treaty of 1950, continued to maintain the formal traditional relations. However, in course of time, the Nepalese stand underwent drastic change, which is evident from the analysis made earlier. Hence, India has to accept it as a psedo-concern or has to live with it like a migraine, for the days to come. This contradiction may continue for sometimes implicitly and sometimes explicitly as well.

The fourth dilemma is the faulty perception of the Indian establishment which always equated Kathmandu and its elite with Nepal. It always tried to please them at any cost neglecting others who really constitue Nepal. If it continues for those who are in power, it is well and good for them and if it deviates from its earlier track by shifting its attention to others, Kathmandu elite will oppose it as has been experienced recently while promulgating the new constitution. Hence, any change in perception will meet with all sorts of opposition and resistance from Kathmandu and will face it in the future too.

The fifth dilemma, which is a corollary of the fourth one, is connected with the inhabitants of Terai/Madhes region who aspired for equality with the hill-origin people. With the people's movements in Nepal, Madhesis and other marginalized communities like Janajatis and Dalits started aspiring for equality with the ruling elite. They are struggling for it against their stiff resistance. It is obvious from the adoption of the new constitution by the constituent assembly half-heartedly leaving room for another struggle. India, if remains neutral, it will be welcomed by the elite and if it shows its sympathy to the Madhesis, it will invite opposition from Kathmandu and its ruling elite.

Sixthly, India faces another dilemma in its diplomatic endeavours in Nepal while dealing with its political players. In the Nepalese politics, there were three factors playing their decisive roles. First, it was Monarchy or its shadow (now), which was sovereign and had effective control over the Kathmandu elite and kept its people suppressed and voiceless. Secondly, the political parties, which came into being in early 1950s, were only after acquiring state power either by pleasing monarchy or opposing it. In their early days, before 1950's armed revolution, all political activities were banned. Similar situation prevailed again after 15 December 1960, when the elected government was dismissed, constitution was suspended, and PM with his cabinet colleagues were arrested and all political activities were banned. It took almost three decades to end the partyless Panchayat system. Thirdly, it is the people whose interests count decisively in a democratic regime. Nepal is a country with more than 120 castes and communities with their mother tongues. It is multicultural, multi-religious, multi-racial and multi-lingual. It is a challenging task to manage the plurality of the country. Sadly, neither the monarchy nor the political parties cared for the people. Significantly, there is no monarchy now. Previously, India had to deal with Monarchy, then it dealt with political parties and now it has to deal with the people. Since Nepal is not a mono-lithic nation, India has to deal with the people who are marginalized. The Kathmandu elite and those who are in power will not tolerate its minimized dominance. Hence, it is a Herculean task before India to have a balanced diplomacy in Nepal. Any hasty and immature diplomacy will prove to be problematic for India.

China Yet Another Factor:

Seventhly, there is yet another factor, which has been resisting the influence of Indian diplomacy, the role of communist China, which emerged as a communist nation in 1949. China captured Tibet in 1959 and declared it later as its autonomous region, perhaps, only for namesake. India always remained defensive in the context of China. Since monarchy and communist regime had one similarity in respect of governance that both preferred centralized, regimented and authoritarian rule, China always stood by the Monarchy, where as India, at least, pretends to stand for its people and democracy. This is the basic difference between the two. China is, therefore, an important factor, which has been playing its role silently and strategically to seek expansion of its share of influence with all its might. In this connection, Lok Raj Baral writes:

"China clout in Nepal seemed to have increased in recent years, while India's role is somewhat declined despite its overarching relations with Nepal"(1) This has actually pushed India to the corner. It is for India to decide whether it has to assert itself suitably or not. Only casual telephonic talks would hardly change the political course.

India is now on the horns of a dilemma, as it is difficult for it to accept the reality as it is and also is not in a position to change it to suit it.

Act Urgently:

It is high time for India to introspect, revise and devise its approaches and action in dealing with it. Nepal appears to be heading gradually towards becoming another Pakistan for India. It is partly due to Indian's approach, partly due to Nepal's internal necessity and partly because of China, which has been showing its economic might in Nepal. It seems that China has been supporting Pakistan against

India in several ways and now it wishes to play Nepal against India. It has now found another friend in Nepal, which is not happy with India.

There are three choices before the policy makers of India. First, try to neutralize the Chinese effect by positive steps. Second, adopt aggressive diplomacy to pressurize the government to listen to the Indian grievances. And lastly, wait and watch how China handles Nepal and how Nepal reciprocates.

India has to introspect over its own policies and performances in Nepal. The deficiency of India's past performance in executing its earlier agreements is another challenge which affects its effective diplomacy in Nepal. There are some misconceptions between them as India could not execute the provisions of the agreements on the two major river projects were signed earlier. The confusion should be cleared as early as possible and the Nepalese claims should be addressed immediately. But the fact remains that the agreements were signed between two countries whereas the execution part was the subject of Indian states that marred the fulfillment of the agreements.

S.D. Muni's elaboration in this regard is very relevant as he writes:

"The central dilemma of the Indo-Nepalese relations is the incompatible nature of the Indian and Nepalese states, due to their respective social characters. Over the years, marginal changes have taken place in the feudal character of the Nepali State as a very small but significant commercial bourgeoisie and middle class is emerging. But this emergence is still taking place under the protective umbrella of the feudal order." (2) He writes significantly:

"Political changes in India have not much to do with the policy towards Nepal and consequently, India-Nepal relations. In a way, India's Nepal policy has always been a matter of debate in the inner policy circles as also at the level of political competition. For instance, during the anti-Rana revolution of 1950-51, Nehru was confronted by two conflicting pressures. One, from the right of the centre, which wanted not to disturb the Ranas and have pragmatic alliance with them to protect India's perceived security interests. The second pressure came from the Congress Socialists, i.e. those taking left of the centre, who asked for all out support for the democratic forces and carry the momentum of change generated in Nepal at that time to the extent of turning the kingdom into a Republic.

These polarities in the Indian political culture have continued to reflect that Nepal-bias for all these years, wherever need for taking position has arisen. These polarities existed even in the Janta government (with its socialist members pushing the government towards greater identification with B.P. Koirala and his Nepal Congress and the traditionalist elements, like the B.J.P. and even Prime Minister Morarji Desai favouring a harmonious relationship with the king), which was otherwise committed to be soft and accommodating towards all the neighbours, including Nepal. This was to underline the Janta government's contrast with Mrs Gandhi's approach and style in dealing with India's neighbours." (3)

Join Hands Together:

Significantly, in the last century, the world gradually turned into a global village and the countries, which fought two World Wars in Europe, joined hands together, although Britain is in the process of pulling out of it. Especially, in the twenty-first century, not only did these countries abolish their visa system for their citizens, they did also introduce a common currency. The Korean peninsula has started dreaming of unified Korea and lasting peace forgetting the war that divided the peninsula into North Korea and South Korea in mid-20eth century. It is the prime duty of the leaders of these two countries to sit together and evolve a common interest strategy to avoid further gap between the two. Otherwise, both the countries have to face ugly situations which they have not visualized. The diplomacy of one country will prove effective, only if, another responses positively.

Reference:

1. Baral, Lok Raj, 2018, Preface to Politics of Geo-Politics: Continuity and Change in India-Nepal Relations, p. viii.
2. Muni, S.D. India and Nepal, 1992, p. 9.
3. Ibid, p.9-10.

❖ ❖ ❖

Bibliography:

Acharya Baburam, 2055(BS) Aba Yasto Kahilyai Nahos, Pulisher, Srikrishna Achrya

Achrya Yagnanath, 2043(BS), 3rd edi. Nepalko Itihasa, Koseli Prakashan, Mahendrapul. Pokhara, Nepal.

Baral. Dr. Loj Raj, 2018, Preface to Politics of Geo-Politics: Continuity of Change in India –Nepal Relations, pub. by Adarsh Books, new Delhi.

Brown Chris & Ainley Kirsten, 2015 Reprint, Understanding International Relations, Fouth Edition, Palgrave Macmillan.

Burghart Richard, 2016, The History of Janakpurdham, edited and introduced by Maretin Gaenszle, Ist edition, Social Science Baha, and Hima Books, Himal Kitab Pvt. Ltd. 521Narayan Gopal Sadak, Lazimpart, Kathmandu-2

Joshi, Ramhari,' Atma Katha Tatha Nepali Conresssanga Gansiyaka Samjhanaharu, The Rising Sun Printers, Teku, Kathmanu, 2067. BS.

Koirala, B.P. Atmavritamta, 2055 BS, Jagadamba Prakashana, Ist edition, Laloitpur, Nepal.

Koirala M.P. 2008, A Role in a revolution,pub. by Jagadamba Prakashan, Patan Dhola, Lalitpur, Nepal.

Krikpatrick William J., 2007, Rupa Co, 7/16, Ansari Road, Daryagunj, New Delhi, 110002

Khanal, Yadu Nath, 1988, Essays in Nepal's Foreign Affairs, pub. By Murari Prasag Upadhyay, Gha 1-29, Kathmandu-2, Nepal.

Leo E. Rose, 1971, South Asia Edition, published by Mandala Book Point, Kantipath, 538, Kathmandu, Nepal.

Levi Sylvain, 1905, Le Nepal: Etude Historique dun Royaume Hindu, Nepali Translation, 5th edition, 2013, Himal Kitab Pvt. Ltd, Narayan Gopal Sadak, Kathmanu-2.

Muni S.D., 1992, India And Nepal, Konark Publishers Pvt Ltd, A-149, Main Vikas Marg, Delhi 110092.

Pradhan Bishwa Prof., 1996, Pub. by Mrs Durga Devi Pradhan, Museum Road, Chhauni, Kathmandu.

Editors-Sangroula, Dr. Yubaraj and Karki Rohit, 2015, Geo-Strategic Challemges to Nepal's Foreign Policy and Way Forward, Pub. by Kathmandu School of Law, Dadhikot- Bhaktapur, Nepal.

Rasgotra, Maharajakrishna, A life in Diplomacy, 2016, First pub. in Viking by Penguin Books India Pvt. Ltd, 7th Floor, Infinity Tower C, DLF Cyber City, Gurgoan 122002, Haryana, India.

Regmi, Mahesh C. 1999, Imperial Gurkha, first edition, Pub. by Adroit Publishers, C-8/2, Yamuna Vihar, Delhi, 110053.

Saran, Shyam, 2017, How India Sees The World, Kautilya to the 21st Century, Juggernot Books, KS House, 118 Shahpur Jat, New Delhi 110049. India

Shaha, Rishikesh, 1992, Nepal's Foreign Policy: Focus on Nepal-India Relations, Pub. under Nepal's India Policy, by CNAS, edi. By Dhruba Kumar, Centre for Nepal and Asian Studies, Tribhuvan University, Kirtipur, Kathmandu Nepal.

News Papers:

1. Republica, English dialy, published from Kathmandu.
2. The Kathmandu Post, English daily, published from Kathmandu.
3. The Rising Nepal, English daily, published from Kathmandu.
4. The Statesman, English daily, published from Delhi and Kolkata (India)

A Collection of Articles:

1. The Open Market(Khula Bazar) Published from Kathmandu.

❖ ❖ ❖

Appendix-1

Treaty of Peace and Friendship
Kathmandu, July 31, 1950

The Government of India and the Government of Nepal, recognising the ancient ties which have happily existed between the two countries for centuries;

Desiring still further to strengthen and develop these ties and to perpetuate peace between the two countries;

Have resolved therefore, to entrer into a treaty of peace and friendship with each other and have, for this purpose, appointed as their plenipotentiaries the following persons, namely,

(i) The government of India :

(ii) His Excellency Shri Chandreshwar Prasad Nirain Singh,

Ambassador of India in Nepal.

The Government of Nepal:

Maharaja Mohun Shamsher Jung Bahadur Rana,
Prime Minister and Supreme Commander-in-Chief of Nepal,
Who having examined each other's credentials and found them good and in due from

Have agreed as follows:

Article I

There shall be everlasting peace and friendship between the

Government of India and the Government of Nepal. The two Governments agree mutually to acknowledge and respect the complete sovereignty, territorial integrity and independence of each other.

Article II

The two Governments hereby undertake to inform each other of any serious friction or misunderstanding with any neighbouring state likely to cause any breach in the friendly relations subsisting between the two Governments.

Article III

In order to establish and maintain the relations referred to in Article I the two Governments agree to continue diplomatic relations with each other by means of represntatives with such staff as is necessary for the due performance of their functions.

The representatives and such of their staff as may be agreed upon shall enjoy such diplomatic privileges and immunities as are customarily granted by international law on a reciprocal basic :

Provided that in no case shall these be less than those granted to persons of a similar status of any state having diplomatic relations with either government.

Article IV

The two governments agree to appoint consuls general, consuls, vice consuls and other consular agents, who shall reside in towns, ports and other places in each other's territory as may be agreed to:

Consuls-general, consuls, vice consuls and consular agents shall be such exequatur or authorization is liable to withdrawn by the country which issued it, if considered necessary. The reasons for the withdrawal shall be indicated wherever possible.

The persons mentioned above shall enjoy on a reciprocal basis all the rights, privileges, exemptions and immunities that are accorded to person of corresponding status of any other state.

Article V

The government of Nepal shall be free to import, from or through the territory of India, arms, ammunition or warlike material and equipment necessary for the security of Nepal. The procedure for giving effect to this arrangement shall be worked out by the two governments acting in consultation.

Article VI

Each government undertakes, in token of the neighborly friendship between India and Nepal, to give to the nationals of the other, in its territory, national treatment with regard to participation in industrial and economic development of such territory and to grant of concessions and contracts relating to such development.

Article VII

The governments of India and Nepal agree to grant, on a reciprocal basis, to the nationals of one country in the territories of the other the same privileges in the matter of residence, ownership of property, participation in trade and commerce, movement and other privileges of similar nature.

Article VIII

So far as matters dealt with herein are concerned, this treaty cancels all previous treaties, agreements and arrangements entered into on behalf of India between the British Government and the Government of Nepal.

Article IX

This treaty shall come into force from the date of signature by both governments.

Article X

This treaty shall remain in force until it is terminated by either party by giving on year's notice.

Done in duplicate at Kathmandu this 31st day of July, 1950.

Sd/-	Sd/-
Chandreshwar Prasad	Mohun Shamsher Jang
Narain Singh	Bahadur Rana
For the government of India	For the government of Nepal

(At a press conference in New Delhi on 3rd December 1959 Prime Minister Jawarharlal Nehru for the first time disclosed that letters were exchanged along with the signing of the treaty which were kept secret. Through these letters have not been officially made public, they have since appeared in a number of texts and are reproduced below. *Editor*)

Letter from the Ambassador of India to the
Prime Minister of Nepal

Kathmandu
Dated the 3th July, 1950

Your Highness!

In the course of our discussion of the treaties of peace and friendship the government of India and the government of Nepal, we agreed that pursuance of this understanding; it is hereby agreed between the two governments:

1. Neither Government shall tolerate any threat to the security of the other by a foreign aggressor. To deal with any such threat, the two governments shall consult with each other and devise effective countermeasures.
2. Any arms, ammunition or warlike material and equipment necessary for the security of Nepal that the government of Nepal may import through the territory of India shall be so imported with assistance and agreement of the Government of India. The Government of India will take steps for the smooth and expeditious transport of such arms and ammunition through India.
3. In regard to Article 6 of the Treaty of Peace and Friendship which provides for national treatment, the government of India recognizes that it may be necessary for some time to come to afford the Nepalese nationals in Nepal protection from unrestricted competition. The nature and extent of this protection will be determined as and when required by mutual agreement between the two governments.
4. If the government of Nepal should decide to seek foreign assistance in regard to the development of the natural resources of, or of any industrial project in Nepal, the Government of Nepal shall give first preference to the government of Nepal shall give first preference to the government or the nationals of India, as the case may be, provided that the terms offered by the government of India or Indian nationals, as the case may be, are not less favorable to Nepal than the terms offered by any other foreign Government or by other foreign nationals. Nothing in the foregoing provision shall apply to assistance that the government of Nepal may seek from the United Nations Organization or any of its specialized agencies.

5. Both governments agree not to employ any foreigners whose activity may be prejudicial to the security of the other. Either government may make representations to the other in this behalf, as or when occasion requires.

Please, accept your highness; the assurances of my highest consideration.

Sd/-
Chandreshwar Prasad Narian Singh
Ambassador Extraordinary and Plenipotenitary
of India at the Court of Nepal.

To

His Highness Mohun Shamsher Jung Bahadur Rana, Maharja,

Prime Minister and Supreme Commander-in-Chief of Nepal.

Letter from the Prime Minister of Nepal to the
Ambassador of India, Kathmandu

Dated the 31st July, 1950

Your Excellency!

In the course of our discussion of the treaties of peace and friendship and of trade and commerce which have been happily concluded between the government of India and the government of Nepal we agreed that certain matters of details be regulated by an exchange of letters. In pursuance of this understanding, it is hereby agreed between the two governments:

1. Neither Government shall tolerate any threat to the security of the other by a foreign aggressor. To deal with any such threat, the two governments shall consult with each other and devise effective countermeasures.

2. Any arms, ammunition or warlike material and equipment necessary for the security of Nepal that the government of Nepal may import through the territory of India shall be so imported with the assistance and agreement of the government of India. The government of India will take steps for the smooth and expeditious transport of such arms and ammunition through India.
3. In regard to Article 6 of the Treaty of Peace and Friendship which provides for national treatment, the government of India recognizes that it may be necessary for some time to come to afford the Nepalese nationals in Nepal protection from unrestricted competition. The nature and extent of this protection will be determined as and when required by mutual agreement between the two governments.
4. If the government of Nepal should decide to seek foreign assistance in regard to the development of the natural resources of or of any industrial project in Nepal, the Government of Nepal shall give first preference to the government or the nationals of India, as the case may be, provided that the terms offered by the government of India or India nationals, as the case may be are not less favorable to Nepal than the terms offered by any other foreign government or by other foreign nationals. Nothing in the foregoing provision shall apply to assistance that the government of Nepal may seek from the United Nations Organization or any of its specialized agencies.
5. Both governments agree not to employ any foreigners whose activity may be prejudicial to the security of the other. Either Government may make representations to the other in this behalf, as or when occasion requires.

Please accept excellency! the assurances of my highest consideration.

Sd/-
Mohun Shamsher Jung Bahadur Rana
Maharaja, Prime Minister and
Supreme Commander-in Chief of Nepal

To: His Excellency Shri Chandreshwar Prasad Narain Singh,
Ambassador Extraordinary and Plenipotentiary of India at the
Court of Nepal, Indian Embassy, Kathmandu.

❖ ❖ ❖

Appendix-2

NEPAL ET ROYAUME-UNI
Traite d'amitie, signe a Khatmandou, le 21 december 1923, et Note de la meme date concernant l'importation des armes et munitions au Nepal.

NEPAL AND UNITED KINGDOM

Treaty of Friendship, signed at Katmandu, December 21, 1923, and Note baring the same Date respecting the Importation of Arms and Ammunition into Nepal.

Societe des Nations — Recueil des Traites.

No. 934. — TREATY[1] OF FRIENDSHIP BETWEEN THE NEPAL AND UNITED KINGDOM, SIGNED AT KATMANDU, DECEMBER 21, 1923, AND NOTE BEARING THE SAME DATE RESPECTING THE IMPORTATION OF ARMS AND AMMUNITION INTO NEPAL.

Texte officiel anglais communiqué par *le Ministire des .Affaires etrangeres de Sa Majeste Britannique. L'enregistrement de ce Traite a eu lieu le 3 aoat* 1925.

TREATY.

Whereas peace and friendship have now existed between the British government and the government of nepal since the signing of the treaty[2] of segowlie on the second day of december one thousand eight hundred and fifteen ; and whereas since that date the Government of Nepal has ever displayed its true friendship for the British Government and the British Government has as constantly shown its goodwill towards the Government of Nepal ; and whereas the Governments of both the countries are now desirous of still further strengthening and cementing the good relations and friendship which have subsisted between them for more than a century ; the two High Contracting Parties having resolved to conclude a new Treaty of Friendship have agreed upon the following articles :

Article 1

There shall be perpetual peace and friendship between the Governments of Great Britain and Nepal, and the two Governments agree mutually to acknowledge and respect each other's independence, both internal and external.

Article 2

All previous Treaties, Agreements and Engagements, since and including the Treaty of Segowlie of 1815, which have been concluded between the two Governments are hereby confirmed, except so far as they may be altered by the present Treaty.

Article 3

As the preservation of peace and friendly relations with the neighboring States whose territories adjoin their common frontiers is to the mutual interests of both the High Contracting Parties, they hereby agree to inform each other of any serious friction or misunderstanding with those States likely to rupture such friendly relations, and each to exert its good offices as far as may be possible to remove such friction and misunderstanding.

1 L'echange des ratifications a eu lieu a Khatmandou le 8 April 1925. De Martens, Nouveau Recueil de Traites, tome II, page 743.

Societe des Nations — Recueil des Traites.

Article 4

Each of the High Contracting Parties will use all such measures as it may deem practicable to prevent its territories being used for purposes inimical to the security of the other.

Article 5

In view of the long standing friendship that has subsisted between the British Government and the Government of Nepal, and for the sake of cordial neighbourly relations between them, the British Government agrees that the Nepal Government shall be free to import from or through British India into Nepal whatever arms, ammunition, machinery, warlike material or stores may be required or desired for the strength and welfare of Nepal, and that this arrangement shall hold good for all time as long as the British Government is satisfied that the intentions of the Nepal Government are friendly and that there is no immediate danger to India from such importations. The Nepal Government, on the other hand, agrees that there shall be no export of such arms, ammunition, etc., across the frontier of Nepal either by the Nepal Government or by private individuals.

If, however, any Convention for the regulation of the Arms Traffic, to which the British Government may be a Party, shall come into force, the right of importation of arms and ammunition by the

Nepal Government shall be subject to the proviso that the Nepal Government shall first become a Party to that Convention, and that such importation shall only be made in accordance with the provisions of that Convention.

Article 6

No Customs duty shall be levied at British Indian Ports on goods imported on behalf of the Nepal Government for immediate transport to that country provided that a certificate from such authority as may from time to time be determined by the two Governments shall be presented at the time of importation to the Chief Customs Officer at the port of import setting forth that the goods are the property of the Nepal Government, are required for the public services of the Nepal Government, are not for the purpose of any State monopoly or State trade, and are being sent to Nepal under orders of the Nepal Government.

The British Government also agrees to the grant in respect of all trade goods, imported at British Indian Ports for immediate transmission to Katmandu without breaking bulk en route of a rebate of the full duty paid, provided that in accordance with arrangements already agreed to between the two Governments, such goods may break bulk for repacking at the port of entry under Customs supervision in accordance with such rules as may from time to time be laid down in this behalf. Rebate may be claimed on the authority of a certificate signed by the said authority that the goods have arrived at Katmandu with the Customs seals unbroken and otherwise untampered with.

Article 7

This Treaty signed on the part of the British Government by Lieutenant-Colonel W. F. T. O'Connor, C.I.E., C.V.O., British Envoy at the Court of Nepal, and on the part of the Nepal Government by General His Highness Maharaja Sir Chandra Shumshere Jung, Bahadur Rana, G.C.B., G.C.S.I., G.C.M.G., G.C.V.O., D.C.L., Thong-lin Pimina-Kokang-Wang-Syan, Prime Minister and 362 Sociite des Nations — Recueil des Traitefs. 1925

Marshal of Nepal, shall be ratified and the ratifications shall be exchanged at Katmandu as soon as practicable. Signed and sealed at Katmandu this the twenty-first day of December in the year one thousand nine hundred and twenty-three anno Domini, corresponding with the sixth Paush, Sambat Era one thousand nine hundred and eighty.

(L. S.) W. F. O'CONNOR. Lieutenant-Colonel, British Envoy at the Court of Nepal.

(L. S.) CHANDRA SHUM SHERE, Prime Minister and Marshal of Nepal.

NOTE. THE PRIME MINISTER OF NEPAL TO THE BRITISH ENVOY AT THE COURT OF NEPAL.

MY DEAR COLONEL O'CONNOR! Regarding the purchase of arms and munitions which the Government of Nepal buys from time to time for the strength and welfare of Nepal, and imports to its own territory from and through British India in accordance with Article 5 of the Treaty between the two Governments, the Government of Nepal hereby agrees that it will, from time to time before the importation of arms and munitions at British Indian Ports, furnish detailed lists of such arms and munitions to the British Envoy at the Court of Nepal in order that the British Government may be in a position to issue instructions to the port authorities to afford the necessary facilities for their importation in accordance with Article 6 of this Treaty.

Sociite des Nations — Recueil des Traitefs. 1925

Marshal of Nepal, shall be ratified and the ratifications shall be exchanged at Katmandu as soon as practicable. Signed and sealed at Katmandu this the twenty-first day of December in the year one thousand nine hundred and twenty-three anno Domini, corresponding with the sixth Paush, Sambat Era one thousand nine hundred and eighty.

(L. S.) W. F. O'CONNOR. Lieutenant-Colonel, British Envoy at the Court of Nepal.

(L. S.) CHANDRA SHUM SHERE, Prime Minister and Marshal of Nepal.

NOTE. THE PRIME MINISTER OF NEPAL TO THE BRITISH ENVOY AT THE COURT OF NEPAL. r

MY DEAR COLONEL O'CONNOR, Regarding the purchase of arms and munitions which the Government of Nepal buys from time to time for the strength and welfare of Nepal, and imports to its own territory from and through British India in accordance with Article 5 of the Treaty between the two Governments, the Govern-ment of Nepal hereby agrees that it will, from time to time before the importation of arms and munitions at British Indian Ports, furnish detailed lists of such arms and munitions to the British Envoy at the Court of Nepal in order that the British Government may be in a position to issue instructions to the port authorities to afford the necessary facilities for their importation in accordance with Article 6 of this Treaty.

Nepal, December 21, 1923.
I am, &c.
To Lieutenant-Colonel W. F. T. O'CONNOR, C.I.E., C.V.O.,
British Envoy at the Court of Nepal.
(Signed) CHANDRA.
NO 934

❖ ❖ ❖

Appendix-3

UNDERSTANDING ON IMPORT OF ARMS BY NEPAL

Royal Nepalese Embassy
Barakhamba Road
New Delhi (India)
January 30, 1965

Your Excellency!

I write to acknowledge the receipt of your letter of today's date, which reads as follows:-

During his visit to Delhi in August, 1963 His Majesty the King of Nepal had raised the question of the reorganisation and modernisation of the Nepalese Army. The Government of India expressed their willingness to provide the necessary assistance, and discussions took place in Delhi in December 1963 between a delegation of His Majesty's Government and representatives of the Government of India, with a view to determining the details of the assistance required by His Majesty's Government for the reorganisation and modernisation of the Nepalese Army.

1. During these discussions, the Nepalese delegation had proposed that the Government of India should assist His Majesty's Government in the raising and equipping of a new brigade group.
2. The Government of India have given full and detailed consideration to the proposals made by His Majesty's Government. In view of the close and traditional bonds of

friendship between the two countries, the Government of India are anxious to give all possible assistance to His Majesty's Government with the object of strengthening the security and independence of Nepal.

3. In the furtherance of these objectives it is hereby agreed that:

   (a) The Government of India undertake to supply arms, ammunition and equipment for the entire Nepalese Army on the basis of a total strength of about 17000 men, comprising four reorganised brigades. This will be inclusive of the existing Himal Troops, Home Guards, Household Troops, Militia companies etc.

   (b) The Government of India further undertake to replace the existing Nepalese stock by modern weapons as soon as available and also to provide the maintenance of and replacement for the equipment to be supplied by them.

   (c) The Government of India undertake to provide all training facilities required for the Nepalese armed forces personnel in the training establishments in India, as necessary, and also by sending training personnel to Nepal at the request of His Majesty's Government. During their training in India adequate funds will be made available by the Government of India to enable them to meet expenses on a parity basis as incurred by the Indian military personnel of equivalent rank. The Government of India will also bear the expenses on account of lodging, including water charges and electricity, of such personnel. During the period of training, Nepalese officers will be given an allowance to enable them to defray the cost of incidental expenses, while other ranks will be provided with free messing.

   (d) The Government of India will give full assistance to His Majesty's Government for the procuring in India, on payment, of olive green drill and other items of clothing and general stores, such as boots and webbing etc. which are required for officers and men of the Nepalese Army.

(e) The existing programme of supplies of military equipment on a credit basis having been completed, the military assistance to be provided by the Government of India under this letter will be on a grant basis.

(f) The equipment and other assistance to be provided by the Government of India will be for the use of the Nepalese Army only, and shall not be diverted to any third party.

(g) The supplies under this programme of assistance will commence as soon as the composition and schedules of supply and the details of pattern and equipment have been agreed upon between the Defense authorities of India and Nepal.

4. The Government of India understand that the Governments of the U.S.A. and the U.K. have also agreed to furnish some defense assistance to His Majesty's Government with a view to supplementing assistance from India. The Governments of the U.K. and the U.S.A. have given the Government of India to understand that if there are any shortfalls in the supply of arms and equipment by the Government of India, these two Governments will fill the gaps to the extent of their ability. At an appropriate time, the details can he suitably coordinated.

5. The arrangements envisaged above shall have no bearing on the independent foreign policy of either Government. The Government of ammunition of warlike material and equipment necessary for the security worked out by the two Governments acting in consultation.

6. The arrangements envisaged in this note may be reviewed from Majesty's Government of Nepal.

7. I shall be grateful if your excellency would kindly confirm that the above correctly sets out the understanding reached between us, and the at this letter together with your excellency's reply will consitute an agreement between his magesty's Government of Nepal and the Government of India which will come into force on the date of your excellency's replay.

   I confirm that the foregoing correctly sets out the understanding reached between us and that your excellency's letter of January 30, 1965 together with this replay constitutes an agreement between his Majesty's Government of Nepal and the Government of India, which comes into force from today, January 30, 1965.

   Please accept, Excellency, the assurances of my highest consideration and esteem.

(S.d) Royal Nepalese Ambassador
His Excellency! Shri Y.D. Gundevia,
Foreigh Secretary to the Govt. of India,
New Delhi.

❖ ❖ ❖

Apendix-4

MEMORANDUM OF AGREEMENT ON RECRUITMENT OF GORKHA TROOPS

At a meeting held at Kathmandu on 1st May 1947 between representatives of His Majesty's Government in the United Kingdom; the Government of India and Government of Nepal, His Highness the Prime Minister and Supreme Commander-in-Chief of Nepal, stated that he would welcome the proposals to maintain the Gurkha connection with the armies of the United Kingdom and India on the following basis "If the terms and conditions at the final stage do not prove detrimental to the interest or dignity of the Nepalese Government, my Government will be happy to maintain connections with both armies, provided men of the Gurkha regiments are willing so to serve (if they will not be looked upon as distinctly mercenary)".

1. Discussions have taken place in Delhi between representatives of His Majesty's Government in the United Kingdom and of the Government of the Dominion of India and the points of agreement are embodied in the Memorandum dated 7th November 1947 a copy of which forms Annexure I of this document. Necessary financial adjustments between the two Governments are still under consideration.
2. Further discussions between the representatives of the three Governments have taken place at Kathmandu during which the Government of Nepal have put forward certain pertinent observations on the memorandum of Agreement referred to in the preceding paragraph which are set out in Annexure II.

In regard to these points, the representatives of His Majesty's Government in the United Kingdom and of the Government of the Dominion of India have replied as follows:-

a) Location of the Recruiting Depots. The use of the existing depots at Gorakhpur and Ghum has been sought by His Majesty's Government in the United Kingdom for a temporary period only pending establishment of their own depots in Nepal. The wishes of the Government of Nepal have been noted and arrangements for the establishment in India of the Recruiting Depots required to meet the needs of the Gurkha units of the British Army will be settled between the United Kingdom and Indian Government.

b) Desire of the Government of Nepal that the total number of Gurkha Units to be employed in the Armies of the United Kingdom and of India shall be limited and brought down to the peace time strength of 20 Battalions out of which 8 Battalions will be allotted to the British Army.

3. The representatives of His Majesty's Government in the United Kingdom and of the Government of Dominion of India have taken note of the wishes of the Government of Nepal.

The representative of His Majesty's Government in the United Kingdom has explained that the long term planning of British Post-War Army has proceeded on the assumption that the Government of Nepal would be prepared to furnish sufficient men to establish the equivalent of an Infantry Division in South-East Asia and he has received an assurance from the Government of Nepal that a final decision on the question of recruitment of Gurkhas in excess of 8 Battalions at peace-time strength shall be left open until

His Majesty's Government in the United Kingdom have had an opportunity of considering the views of the Government of Nepal.

As regards the reduction of the Gurkha Units in the Indian Army the Government of Nepal have informed the representative of the Government of the Dominion of India that the reduction should not be carried out immediately in view of the existing political situation in India.

(c) Arrangements for the import of the foreign currency belonging to the Gurkha units of the 8 Battalions serving overseas.

It is noted that the Government of the Dominion of India has agreed to afford all normal facilities in regard to the import of foreign currency belonging to these men (Annexure I, item 10). A reply to the specific point raised in this connection will be sent to the Government of Nepal in due course.

4. The Government of Nepal being generally satisfied in regard to the terms and conditions of employment of Gurkha troops and taking note of the agreement dated 7th November 1947 reached between His Majesty's Government in the United Kingdom and of the Government of Dominion of India hereby signify their agreement to the employment of Gurkha troops in the armies of the United Kingdom and of India.
5. In addition to the observations referred to above the Government of Nepal have put forward certain suggestions connected with the employment of Gurkhas in the armies of the United Kingdom and of India. These suggestions are contained in Annexure III of this document and the views of the two Governments thereon will be communicated to the Government of Nepal in due course.
6. Note has been taken of the desire of His Majesty's Government in United Kingdom that prompt action be taken to ascertain

the wishes of the personnel of the 8 Gurkha Battalions concerned as to whether they desire to be transferred for service under the United Kingdom Government. With this object in view a questionnaire and a Memorandum embodying terms and conditions of service have been prepared by the representatives of His Majesty's Government in the United Kingdom. These documents are acceptable to the Government of India and Nepal. They will be issued to the personnel of the 8 units concerned as soon as possible. In accordance with the wishes of the Government of Nepal as well as those of the Government of India it is agreed that their representatives will be present with the 8 units while the referendum is being taken.

7. The representatives of the three Governments desire to place on record that their deliberations have been conducted in an atmosphere of cordiality and goodwill and are confident that the friendly relations which have existed in the past will be further cemented as a result of the arrangements which have been agreed for the continued employment of Gurkha soldiers in the armies of the United Kingdom and of India.

8. Signed in triplicate at Kathmandu this 9th day of November; 1947.

(Sd.) A.C.B. SYMON
For the Government of United Kingdom.
(Sd.) BEDI
For the Government of the Dominion of India
(Sd.) PADMA SHAM SHERE JUNG R.B. For the Government of Nepal

❖ ❖ ❖

Annexure I

MEMORANDUM OF AGREEMENT BETWEEN THE GOVERNMENT OF THE DOMINION OF INDIA AND H.M. GOVERNMENT IN THE UNITED KINGDOM

That all volunteers from Regular battalions of each of the second, sixth, seventh and tenth Gurkha Rifles, together with personnel of their regimental centers, shall be transferred to H.M. British Army, subject to the negotiation of terms and conditions with the Government of Nepal.

That the personal arms and equipment of those units if required by H.M. Government will be issued on payment and removed overseas with the units.

That H.M. Government may for the present continue to use the existing recruiting depots at Gorakhpur and Ghum, and that the British and Gurkha military personnel serving in them may wear uniform.

1. That the plans of H.M. Government for recruiting in Nepal up to a possible strength of a Division (say 25,000 men), shall not in any way interfere with recruitment to the Gurkha units in the Indian Army.
2. That Gurkha Officers, recruits, soldiers, ex-soldiers and pensioners of Gurkha units serving H.M. Government, and their dependents, shall be permitted to travel freely between Nepal and an Indian port on their lawful occasions, provided mufti is worn in transit through India; the stipulation

regarding dress shall not apply to the four Regiments named above during their removal from India.

3. That the normal road and rail transport facilities in India shall be available, at the public rates prevailing from time to time, to all British Officers serving with Gurkhas, Gurkha Officers and their families, Gurkha other ranks and their families and the necessary maintenance stores and baggage of such personnel in the service of H.M. Government; and that such staging facilities as may be required shall be provided at the expense of H.M. Government.

4. That India's postal, money-order and telegraphic services to and from Nepal shall be available to H.M. Government, and Gurkhas serving H.M. Government, at the normal rates prescribed from time to time.

5. That the Government of India shall make available annually to 11.M. Government, for the use of Gurkha soldiers, the following quantities of food stuffs:

   a. Atta 2,200 tons

   b. Ghee 750 tons

   c. Dhal 1,200 tons

   d. Condiment Powder 150 tons

   provided H.M. Government arrange to supply the Government of India with 2,200 tons of wheat in replacement of the supplied to them.

6. That the Government of India shall make available to H.M. Government such Indian currency as may be necessary for purposes connected with their employment of Gurkha soldiers, provided that the sterling equivalent thereof shall be credited to the Government of India Sterling Account One.

7. That Gurkha Officers, soldiers, ex-soldiers, pensioners and their dependents shall have the right to send or take Indian money back to Nepal subject only to such Indian currency regulations of general application as may be in force from time to time; foreign currency imported into India shall be subject to the general Indian currency regulations obtaining from time to time.
8. That the basic rates of pay admissible to Gurkha Officers and soldiers serving H.M. Government shall approximate to those laid down in the present Indian Pay Code, at which rates personnel serving at the recruiting depots in Gorakhpur and Ghum shall be paid: and that a special allowance, to compensate for permanent service overseas and high cost of living, shall in addition be admissible to Gurkha Officers and soldiers serving H.M. Govern-men! overseas.
9. Alter the 8 Battalions have been asked to opt for service under 11.M. Government, Government of India will try to make up the deficiency caused by those who do not wish to serve with H.M. Government, by asking other soldiers who have completed their existing engagement and who do not wish to continue to serve in the. Indian Army Units. If the required number cannot thus be made good the deficiency will be made up by H.M. Government by direct recruitment.

(Sd.)	(Sd.)
For the Government of the Dominion of India	For His Majesty's Government in the United Kingdom

❖ ❖ ❖

Annexure II

NEPALESE REACTION TO "POINTS OF AGREEMENT BETWEEN GOVERNMENT OF INDIA AND H.M.G."

1. *Para (3)* It appears that the arrangement of having recruiting Depots at Gorakhpur and Ghum for the British Gurkha Regiments has as an after-thought been made of a temporary character. Nepal Government feels that it would definitely be more convenient to all three parties, if the recruiting is carried on for both Indian and British Armies at the present depots or any other places in India.
2. *Para (4)* In view of our long-standing friendship the Government of Nepal had agreed to raise the strength of the Gurkha Regiments during the period of the last war. But she feels that the continuation of this emergency measure will be too much of a drain on the man-power of the country. So she desires that the total be limited and brought down to the peace-time strength of 20 battalions to be divided between the Indian anntis Armies, as already arranged.
3. *Para (10)* Nepal Government desires that OT origin currency brought by the personnel of the Gurkha Regiments serving abroad be credited to the Nepal Government account in any bank (to be settled afterwards); the Government of Nepal providing Indian currency therefor at the prevailing market

Annexure III

1. In all matters of promotion, welfare and other facilities the Gurkha troops should be treated on the same footing as the other units in the parent army so that the stigma of "mercenary troops" may for all time be wiped out. These troops should be treated as a link between two friendly countries.
2. The Gurkha troops should be given every facility so that it might be officered by their own men and they should be eligible to commissioned ranks with no restrictions whatsoever to the highest level to which qualified officers may be promoted.
3. The Gurkha troops should not be used against Hindu or any other unarmed mobs.
4. To avoid any clash between the Gurkhas themselves, Gurkha troops should not be used if any contingency of their having to serve in opposite camps arises.
5. To enable us supply better quality men, we request that our following military needs may be met:
   i. A well-equipped arms and ammunition factory producing all modern small arms and ammunitions.
   ii. A few Army transport planes.
   iii. Our requirements of Army Stores and civil supplies could be discussed later on.
6. To establish better liaison between Nepal and the troops liaison officers would be appointed by the Nepalese Government and would form part of the unit of the Gurkha troops.

7. It is very desirable that the morale of the recruits as well as the armed forces, should remain unimpaired. Therefore all activities prejudicial to the interest and security of one party should be prevented in the territories of the other parties.
8. The Government of Nepal reserves the right to withdraw all Gurkha troops in case Nepal is involved in any war.
9. All facilities for the training of Nepalese officers in the military academies of India and British should be provided as and when the Nepal Government wants.
10. As Khukri is the religious and national emblem of the Gurkhas forming also a part of the uniform of the Gurkha Army, the carrying of Khukri by Gurkhas of all categories must not be banned in territories where the Gurkhas reside.
11. When Gurkha troops go on active service, intimation might be given to the Government of Nepal.
12. The above mentioned points are to be incorporated in a treaty and or agreement t to be signed between the parties in due course.

❖ ❖ ❖